Richard Wagner
A PORTRAIT

Lennart Svensson

MANTICORE BOOKS
WWW.MANTICOREBOOKS.NET

RICHARD WAGNER-A PORTRAIT

LENNART SVENSSON

COPYRIGHT © LENNART SVENSSON, MANTICORE BOOKS

All rights reserved, no section of this book may be utilized without permission, including electronic reproductions without the permission of the authors or publisher.

BIC Classification:
BGL (Biography: Literary), BGH (Biography: Historical), AVH (Individual Composers), AVGC4 (Classical Music)

978-0-9942525-1-7

MANTICORE BOOKS
www.manticorebooks.net

Table of Contents

Introduction   7

1. BIOGRAPHY   10
Student. Musician. Dresden Calls. Left-Wing Nationalism. Tannhäuser. Revolution. Exile. Forty. The Wagnerian Project. Success. The Ring

2. THE FAIRIES (1833)   28
Composition History. The Plot. Coherence

3. RIENZI, THE LAST OF THE TRIBUNES (1842)   32
Origins. Melodrama. Power Struggle. Populist Ruler

4. THE FLYING DUTCHMAN (1843)   37
Background. A Symbol of the Artist. Sandvik. Daland. Senta. Finale

5. TANNHÄUSER (1845)   45
Origins. Poetic Hero. The Music

6. LOHENGRIN (1850)   48
Arthurian Legend. Synopsis. Bridal Chorus. Monsalvat. The Music of Lohengrin

7. WIELAND THE SMITH (1850)   54

8. TRISTAN AND ISOLDE (1865)   57
Background. The Plot. Love Meeting

9. THE MASTER-SINGERS OF NUREMBERG (1868)   62
Medieval Nuremberg. The Model Master-Singer. Evening. St John's Day. Views. Thomas Mann

10. THE RING OF THE NIBELUNG (1876)   71
Background. The Work. An Overview. Interpretations. Circles of Existence. Wotan. Alberich. In the Eye of the Ring. Nibelungs. Balance. Wotan's Qualms. Key Scene. The Rhine Gold. Outside Valhalla. Nifelhem. Erda's Advice. The Valkyrie. Bride and Sister. Punishment. Siegfried. Fafner. Invoking Erda. Fateful Meeting. Twilight of the Gods. Happenings. The Gibichungs. The Hunt. Flames. The Music. Gods on Stage. Odin. Tolkien

11. PARSIFAL (1882)   111
Medieval Epic Poem. Symbolism. The Grail. The Quest. Kundry. The Spear. Final Act. Healing the Wound. Parsifal on the Met. Controversy. Heroism and Christianity

12. WAGNER AND NIETZSCHE   127
Villa Triebschen. Bayreuth. The Case of Wagner. Put in Perspective

13. ON WAGNER IN D'ANNUNZIO'S *THE FLAME OF LIFE*   134
Giancolo. Monteverdi. The Masterpiece. Wagner Downtown

| 14. ON COMPOSING DRAMAS ABOUT SAINTS | 140 |

| 15. ON BEING CONTROVERSIAL | 142 |

A Pamphlet. Chauvinism. A Politician. Joachim Fest. Similarities. Histrionics. Wagner DNA. Being Pro and Being Anti

| 16. FRANCO-PRUSSIAN WAR | 155 |

Kaisermarsch. The War. Ludwig. Herrenchiemsee

| 17. WAGNER AND POPULAR CULTURE | 162 |

Popular Appeal. Helicopters on the Cover. Excalibur. Film Music. A Novel

| 18. ON BEING A GENIUS | 169 |

Hans Sachs. The Cult. To Be an Artist. The Muses

| 19. SCENOGRAPHY | 174 |

Parsifal on the Moon. Costume Design. Updating Tradition

| 20. ON WAGNER'S MUSIC | 180 |

| 21. WAGNER AND LITERATURE | 183 |

Musical Novels. Explaining the Plot. Tolkien. Mime Artist. The Poet. 51%

| 22. MISCELLANEOUS | 189 |

On Sources, Translations and Spelling   *193*

About the Author   *197*

INTRODUCTION

I was about eight or nine years by then. Living in the northern Swedish town of Örnsköldsvik my older brother had the habit of buying the comic book *Fantomen* (*The Phantom*). Some time during 1974 this comic book ran a series on the inside of the covers, the smooth paper allowing for the reproduction of some alluring pictures, a series retelling the story of Wagner's *The Ring of the Nibelung*. Here it was called "The Legend of the Rhine Gold". And I literally devoured this sequence of miniaturized oil-paintings telling me about Alberich, the theft of the gold, the Aesir in turn snatching it from him, the giant Fafner, Siegfried and all.

This illustrated classic caught the gist of the legend. In retrospect I might say, "it was even better than Wagner", like being able to show Alberich transforming into a giant, fire-breathing dragon. I mean, on stage there is always some form of compromise but as for this comic strip and this particular scene, the incandescent red-and-yellow flames, the poisonous green of the dragon's scales and the sheer size of the dragon, making Wotan and Loke look insignificant—this made an impression. As did many other scenes from the epic, such as the sleeping Brünhilde encircled by flames, Mime's smithy and Siegfried approaching Fafner's rocky desert dwelling.

The introduction of this comic book series mentioned Richard Wagner's name. Thus a seed was planted in me. Some years later I bought a CBS record entitled *Wagner's Greatest Hits* with standards like "Bridal Chorus from Lohengrin", "Master-Singers Overture" and "Ride of the Valkyries". By then I knew something about classical music but the typical classical piece, the works of "absolute music", of

"Opus 10 in D minor" just didn't turn me on. Wagner was a different affair, his music embodying stories, emotions and characters I could more easily relate to.

Another best-of collection on cassette told me more about the Wagner mood. And a 90's university course in cultural studies highlighted the Tristan chord from *Tristan and Isolde*; when I got home from one particular lecture the cassette with the Tristan overture and "Isolde's Love-Death" was salvaged from the depths of my collection and I began to understand the specificity of this music, previously deemed as uninteresting by me. I was more of a *Ring of the Nibelung*-man until then.

As a cultural phenomenon Wagner now is established as mainstream. True, sometimes his controversial sides are in the spotlight. But I have nothing against that. That's how it should be: Wagner had controversial views and they should be discussed.

So then: I'm a Wagner fan of sorts. Among classical composers Wagner is the one that's meant most to me. And this is a book about him, Richard Wagner (1813-1883), the German composer and dramatic artist. On the following pages I will treat his biography, his central works, and I will look into certain aspects of him and his *oeuvre*, like the popular cultural aspect and what it means to be a genius. And—as intimated—what it means to be controversial.

Wagner is, and shall be, held responsible for what he said and wrote. Apart from that it can be said that he played many roles during his life. There were many sides to the man: genius composer, dramatist, polemic pamphleteer, radical revolutionary, liberal nationalist, conservative. The most important role of these is that of the artist. We don't always see that. And for this Wagner himself partly is to blame. For instance, the composer at the end of his life encouraged the tendencies of making himself into a monument. In the 1870's, presiding at his own opera house in Bayreuth, for example, he insisted on being called "master". The ultimate symbol of this monument-making is the Wagner statue in Berlin, inaugurated in 1903.

However, my ambition with this study might be this: having people to look beyond Wagner's character of monument, of a brazen statue looking sternly at you. Along with his less inspiring sides, my aim with this book is to make people see *Wagner the artist* who created worlds of enduring beauty and fascination. With his music dramas Wagner has conquered a whole world and it didn't come easily. I don't mean that we should pity him for the hardships he met along the way, but I do want to paint a portrait of an artist intuitively following his own path, in the process painting landscapes of romance, drama, revolt, passion and spiritual fulfilment. I want to delve into his operas, I want to muse over the plots and reflect over the music *per se*.

Overall Wagner's *oeuvre* is complex. Today's intellectuals don't always get that, being as they are somewhat uneducated, tending to see in only black and white. They are stuck in the iron grip of dualism. For instance, how many know that Wagner was a left-wing revolutionary in the 1849 Dresden upheaval? Also, apart from intellectuals, the easy-going art-lover of today, the opera fan living happily among his Wagner CD's and DVD's, might need to look into the "radical conservative" side of Wagner. No other composer of those days wrote polemical pamphlets of the kind Wagner did. So for them, and all others—Wagner lovers, the culturally interested everyman, intellectuals, all—I give you this Wagner biography, a portrait of a fascinating artist, a controversial polemicist and a living, breathing human being.

Härnösand, November 15, 2014

LENNART SVENSSON

1. BIOGRAPHY

ichard Wagner was born in Leipzig, Saxony, in May 1813. Later he wrote this comic poem about the event:

Im wunderschönen Monat Mai
kroch Richard Wagner aus dem Ei.
Es wünschten viele, die ihn lieben,
er wäre besser drin geblieben.

A prose translation of this might be:

> In the lovely month of May Richard Wagner broke out of the egg. Many who loved him wished that he had stayed in there.

And the meaning? It refers to the critics who later waged a cultural war against Wagner. Wagner was controversial then as now.

As for Richard's father, Carl Friedrich Wagner, he was a police actuary, a sort of civil servant. He died of typhus later in 1813, in November. So you could say that the young Richard was almost fatherless. And in his operas can be found many a young hero who has lost his father: Siegmund in *The Valkyrie*, Siegfried in the eponymous opera, Adriano in *Rienzi* and the protagonist in *The Fairies*, returning to his land after the father has died and by which the action takes off.

Richard's mother, Johanna Rosine Wagner, would live on until the mid 1800's. Later she remarried, going down the aisle with Ludwig

Geyer, a fairly well-known actor who also sang, wrote, and painted. Geyer had been a friend of the Wagners for a long time and there are suspicions that he was the father of Richard. However, on his deathbed Carl Friedrich acknowledged that he himself was the father, and this also seems to be the view held by modern researchers. Richard first bore the surname Geyer but changed it to Wagner in 1827.

Geyer is said to have taught young Richard to draw, paint, and to produce stage plays. Johanna, for her part, rented out rooms to composers, authors, and actors. They now lived in Dresden, the capital of Saxony. Wagner was the youngest of nine brothers and sisters; they sometimes too went into "showbiz" but for this story they aren't important. As for Wagner's musical talent, it took some time to mature. He didn't shine as a child prodigy in this respect like Mozart, Beethoven, or Handel. Wagner also preferred playing by ear to playing by notes. He was a budding genius who knew his worth but he never learned to play piano properly; this he later admitted himself.

In Dresden, at the age of 9, Wagner had a defining experience: he saw Carl Maria von Weber (1786-1826) conduct his opera *Der Freischütz* (*The Marksman*), which had premièred in Berlin the year before, 1821. It was the first opera that utilized a German, medieval setting as well as hints of German folk music in the score. This made a lasting impression on the nascent composer. Wagner wanted to be that man in the pulpit, conjuring up the magic of music and drama. The *northernness* and archaic feeling of it all was something new in the opera world and Wagner would later try to capture this spirit, his crowning achievement being *The Ring of the Nibelung*.

STUDENT

According to Lundewall the young student Wagner was uninterested in most school subjects, except for Greek mythology and history. Wagner also liked literature of the narrative kind. At times he lived with his uncle Adolf with whom he discussed the works of Shakespeare,

Goethe, and Schiller. Wagner became steeped in contemporary and classic German culture, music-wise he was eventually affected by the works of Bach, Mozart, and Beethoven. There was a certain *pathos* in this young man, Wagner.

Wagner's first artistic efforts were in the realm of drama proper, not music. His first opus was the play *Leubald*, a tragedy influenced by Shakespeare and Goethe. Being a bit violent and melodramatic it was, at the same time, a fine effort by a 14 year old. Wagner then realized that the drama could have been better with music underlining and explaining the plot. At the age of 16 he therefore decided to become a composer, taking up his musical studies with renewed fervour. First he borrowed a book on music theory. Then, around 1830, he attended a course in harmony with Christian Gottlieb Müller. In Müller's company Wagner became impressed by Beethoven's 9th symphony and Mozart's *Requiem*.

In 1831 Wagner went to Leipzig university. Here he had lessons with Theodor Weinlig, a church cantor who was impressed by his student; it's said that Weinlig refused any payment for his lessons. The lessons went on for about a year and were somewhat informal in character. The teacher for example let his student compose variations of known works, a natural way of getting to know the works and eventually analyze them. Weinlig also taught Wagner about Bach and how to write a fugue, the result of which later could be seen in the overture to *The Master-Singers of Nuremberg*.

At about 1833 Wagner started to compose his first opera, the unfinished *Die Hochzeit*. Later the same year he made his first completed opera, *The Fairies*. This wasn't staged until 1888, after Wagner's death.

MUSICIAN

When Wagner was 20 he was a skilled musician, not yet a genius composer, but he could earn his living in this trade. He was a "maestro", he could conduct a symphony orchestra. For example, in 1833 he was choir master in Würzburg, northern Bavaria, and in

1834 he was musical director at the opera of Magdeburg, Saxony-Anhalt. By this time he wrote *Das Liebesverbot,* an opera based on Shakespeare's *Measure for Measure.* It was staged in Magdeburg in 1836 but was a failure, being only performed once.

In 1837 Wagner was musical director at the Riga opera by the Batltic Sea, the city by then belonging to The Russian Empire. Today Riga is the capital of Latvia. Now Wagner was married to the singer Minna Planer, the beginning of a troubled relationship that nonetheless lasted for many years. Wagner had a tendency to live expensively and the pair eventually had to flee Riga in order to avoid their creditors. The sea journey was stormy and they had to seek port in Norway, a real-life scene that Wagner later used for the first scene of *The Flying Dutchman.* The Wagners next went to London. Wagner wanted to meet the author Edward Bulwer-Lytton (1803-1873) and show him the *libretto* he had written on the Englishman's novel about Rienzi, the last of the Italian tribunes. But the author wasn't home; it was late summer 1839, the dead season, so no notables were in town. Thus the Wagners soon left for France and Paris, where they stayed 1839-1842.

DRESDEN CALLS

Wagner had no worldly success while in Paris these years. He wrote articles and composed trifles while working on his first operas, *Rienzi* and *The Flying Dutchman*. Even some years later, in 1861, when Wagner's opera *Tannhäuser* was staged in Paris, the success stayed away. The French capital just didn't get this story about choosing the chaste woman above the seductress. The French of those days loved *Grand Opéra*, a crowd-pleasing form of music drama. Wagner's serious approach to art, guided by artists like Shakespeare, Goethe, Bach and Beethoven, just didn't gel with the festivitas and *gaiete* of 19th century Paris. True, Paris was the artistic capital of Europe, every European writer, painter, or composer wanted to make it there, but the style of mid 19th century Paris was a different one from the artistic mood of

Wagner. Only later would Wagner's work be accepted and loved by the French. Admittedly, this process got going in his own lifetime.

While in Paris Wagner completed the above mentioned operas, *Rienzi* and *The Flying Dutchman*. And amid all the misery he got *Rienzi* accepted by the Court Theatre in Dresden. In April 1842 Wagner was able to return home to Germany. He later wrote about the trip: "For the first time I saw the Rhine; with happy tears in my eyes, I, poor artist, swore my German fatherland eternal fidelity."[1]

Wagner lived in Dresden 1842-49, eventually getting the position as Royal Saxon Court Conductor. The chief reason for moving there was that the Court Theatre accepted *Rienzi* for performance, and then other musical jobs followed naturally. Wagner had two other operas staged in Dresden, *The Flying Dutchman* and *Tannhäuser*.

LEFT-WING NATIONALISM

As for Wagner's Dresden years some notes on politics must be made.

In Dresden Wagner eventually took part in the 1848 German revolution. And he did it as a nationalist. This was highly controversial because German nationalism at the time was genuinely anti-establishment. From 1815 to 1848, and even beyond it, some time before the establishment of the German Empire in 1871 after Prussia's victory against France, nationalism in Germany was a freedom movement, a populist cultural and political struggle that met with resistance from the current rulers. By this time the rulers lived in the Congress of Vienna system with cooperating reactionary monarchies (Russia, Prussia, Austria, and France).

If you were a German nationalist in this context you could be imprisoned and have your entire life ruined. So Wagner put a lot on the line when he took part in the revolution. He was then, in 1848, as we have seen, an established Court Conductor and composer with the operas *Rienzi*, *The Flying Dutchman* and *Tannhäuser* behind him.

---

[1] Quoted after Jeanson, p.72; translated by the author.

Being a nationalist and an artist at that time wasn't easy. Wagner had to define what national art was. And he wanted to portray German fairytale and legends on stage, as a new form of musical theatre. It wouldn't do (as with *Rienzi*) to keep on with the current, crowd-pleasing style that the German composer Meyerbeer excelled in. Opera was an established art form at the time but Wagner wanted to renew it in different ways. And with the German approach he believed that one must break up the opera's accepted forms (with elements such as defined vocal numbers) in favour of a more sweeping, broad painting. In particular, Wagner was his own lyricist (librettist) and this both made his project easier and more ambitious; I'd say, more authentic. By then it was the rule for a composer to hire a librettist to have a storyline to compose around. But Wagner himself was a gifted author, being able to write both music and lyrics. Then it became a work at a higher level, a *Gesamtkunstwerk* ("an all-encompassing work of art").

TANNHÄUSER

Wagner's third opera, *Tannhäuser,* was performed in Dresden in 1845. It wasn't exactly a success. But Wagner was employed as Court Conductor and could go on living as before. In 1847 he had completed yet another mythic opera, *Lohengrin*, based on a folk tale about a Grail knight who rescues a princess from a plot. He saves her on the condition that she doesn't ask who he is and when she finally asks, he must say it and leave. The tragedy aside, it shows the capacity of Grail legends to be staged for modern people, telling them something. Wagner returned to the Grail theme in *Parsifal* in the 1870's.

Lohengrin was never performed in Dresden. Wagner then started to write a piece modelled on The Poetic Edda and Nibelungenlied starring Sigurd Fafnesbane, Norse gods and all. At the same time (1848-49) political realities knocked on the door and Wagner's life was turned upside down. It was the revolution that reached Saxony and the rest of Germany. The unrest began in France in February 1848, where the monarchy they had since 1830 was toppled to be replaced by a republic. In the German revolts republicanism and nationalism were to go hand in hand. And individuals such as Wagner were drawn into the fray, with artistic ideas being an integral part of it. Jeanson states:

> The ideals of a new, sound art, which occurred to him [Wagner] could, according to his beliefs, only be achieved through social reform or even revolution. Therefore, he devoted himself to the revolutionary current, which in Dresden got its violent but quickly suppressed eruption with the May revolt of 1849... [2]

At the time Wagner was definitely revolutionary. The Siegfried he wanted to portray was a folk hero in a struggle against the curse of gold. Siegfried wins the Rhine Gold but the treasure is a symbol of greed and capitalism and leads Siegfried, the symbol of the German people, to destruction. That is how Wagner himself saw it.[3] It sounds a bit facile but it isn't totally far-fetched. As long as you don't completely reduce The Ring into a modern, economic drama, into being all about capitalism and workers, then it's legit to see the tale from this aspect. This gives it extra depth. G. B. Shaw for his part later based his leftist interpretation of The Ring on this.[4] The Siegfried legend is complex and can be interpreted in different ways and The Ring, being a modern, variegated work of art, allows this.

After the exile from Dresden Wagner became less political. But once he was clearly in the radical camp and you can't completely wash away this aspect of the Wagnerian psyche. If man escapes from the curse of gold then a new, truer art and a new culture could emerge, as the revolutionary Wagner meant. People will take power back from the aristocracy. Back to nature was also a leitmotif of Wagner at this time. It was utopian thinking in a time of revolt and rebellion.

But Wagner wasn't only a revolutionary theoretician: "He was a member of the democratic *Vaterlandsverein*, delivered fiery speeches,

---

[2] Ibid p.76; translated by the author.
[3] Ibid p.77.
[4] See chapter 10.

socialized with known revolutionaries and participated actively in the May upheaval."⁵ According to Wikipedia Wagner among others met the Russian anarchist Mikhail Bakunin (1814-1876). The same source talks about Wagner being influenced by the ideas of Pierre-Joseph Proudhon, a French anarchist (1809-1865). In short, Wagner was opposed to the current regime, the Saxon kingdom, at the same time as he was employed as Court Conductor. So when the revolt failed Wagner must flee from Dresden.

But I'm getting ahead. Let's look at the events proper in Dresden 1848-49 with Wagner in focus.

REVOLUTION

As mentioned above the French revolt sparking this all-European turmoil started in February 1848. Anti-monarchic, republican sentiments then spread to Germany. The riots in Berlin in March for example were notable, in some cases being more violent than those in Paris. When the dust had settled a political process started in the separate German states, ending in the assembly of a constitutional parliament in Frankfurt. Thus the revolutionary sentiments had born fruit, thus the people would have its say against the princes and kings, but in an orderly fashion.

Exactly what riots did or did not take place in Dresden by this time I don't know. But revolution was in the air and Wagner and the Dresden intelligentsia was drawn along. Wagner, being of a fiery, flippant, easily moved nature got something of a creative boost in speculating about the artistic meaning of the revolution (q.v. the pamphlet *Art and Revolution* from 1849). Whether he was right or wrong in his ideas you must admit that he didn't sit idle and smoke his pipe while this went on. Wagner was no saint: for instance, as Mayer intimates, he might have seen the revolution mainly as a means of realizing his own, earlier held ideas of a new art form. Anyhow, the

---

⁵ Ibid p.77.

phenomenon *art, Germany and Wagner* went through a sort of vortex in 1848-49 that is impossible to ignore when studying his biography, whatever you make of the sincerity of the ideas Wagner discussed. At least it can be noted that the revolution and the following exile didn't stifle his creativity.

Wagner didn't stand on the barricades every day, didn't sit around in revolutionary circles discussing ideas all the time. Dresden and Saxony lived on, mostly as before during this year of revolution. Wagner earned his living as a *maestro* at the royal opera. True, his own operas *Rienzi, Tannhäuser* and *Lohengrin* were unperformed in those days. But he had the time to go to Vienna in 1848 and see the effects of the revolution there. He also visited Weimar and Franz Liszt, a fellow German composer (1811-1886).

Then came May 1849, with riots in Dresden. Mayer gives the background: the parliament in Frankfurt had eventually announced the adoption of a new constitution for Germany. However, the head of the leading German state Prussia, Friedrich Wilhelm IV, had declined the *kaiser* crown for a unified German state that the parliament had offered him. The king of Saxony went along with this "reactionary" line and stated that the proposed constitution had been rejected.

With this the Dresden revolutionaries, among them Wagner, had to act, else their ideas for a unified Germany with the people at the power (under a benevolent monarch) and a new, free art, would melt away like a snowball in hell. An armed rising thus started in Dresden May 4th. The insurgents took over central Dresden and had barricades built by an architect. Wagner himself served as a spotter in a church tower. The Saxon government called for Prussian troop aid. Eventually the capital, Dresden, was attacked by Prussian and Saxon troops. Michail Bakunin, whom Wagner had met, exercised command over the barricades, the sturdy Russian with his healthy beard made an impression on everyone.

By May 9th the opera house was burning and all was lost. The insurgents retreated to a place called Freiberg, Wagner and Minna going there by one-horse cart. Then the company retreated further, to the city of Chemnitz. The other insurgents reached the town earlier than Wagner and were all arrested, among them Bakunin. But Wagner, being late, thus escaped the eye of the authorities. Thus he could go west, leaving Saxony altogether and go to Liszt in Weimar, Thuringia. A "wanted" message went out saying that the 37-38 year old, of middle length and brown hair, glass-eye wearing Richard Wagner should be arrested. But Wagner, leaving Minna behind in Germany (she was not wanted), eventually made his way to Switzerland. What had saved him from being caught during the trip was, for instance, a passport he had been given by a friend, a professor Widmann of Jena. Therefore he could travel under an alias.

EXILE

Wagner was safely on Swiss soil. For a while he thought about moving on to Paris, but eventually he settled in Switzerland. He was now an exile but lived fairly well, being helped with money and accommodation by friends. He was still married to Minna and she joined him in his exile later, but he had little in common with her at this time; this we know from Wagner's autobiography, *Mein Leben*. As for Wagner's reading, it could be said that an acquaintance around this time told him to read Schopenhauer; his use of Buddhism inspired quietism (still your desires) and gave Wagner certain artistic impulses. But as a German nationalist Wagner now had been banished from Eden: he must stay away from all German territory until 1861. Had he returned to Germany anytime in the 1850's he would have been arrested on the spot.

The Swiss years were spent in many ways, within the framework of having to wait for things to get better politically and artistically. Apart from *Lohengrin* being staged in Germany in 1850 there was no worldly success for Wagner during this decade. He lived on loans and gifts from friends and wrote pamphlets on art and music. Wagner began to separate from Minna and had a relationship with Mathilde Wesendonck, a married woman.

Actually this Wesendonck affair went on while he still lived with Minna. Wagner was something of a philanderer with a predilection for extra-marital affairs. Other married women he "scandalized" from now on were Jessie Laussot, Blandine Ollivier and Cosima von Bülow. The upside of this was that he knew what he wrote about when it came to love. Much later (1870) Wagner married this Cosima (1837-1930), Liszt's extra-marital daughter with the countess d'Agoult. Wagner had first seen her in Paris 1853 when she was 16. Cosima was artistically gifted, had a peculiar beauty and a rather fierce nature, it's said. With Cosima Richard had his son Siegfried, who eventually became director of the Festival Theatre in Bayreuth.

But I'm getting ahead. Let's take a closer look at Wagner's Swiss stay in the 1850's with Mayer as the main source. In 1849-51 Wagner wrote programmatic works, essays discussing his ideas on art like *Art and Revolution* and *Artwork of the Future* (both 1849). Then, thanks to Liszt, *Lohengrin* was premièred on the Hoftheater in Weimar in August 1850. It was something of a success. Wagner now lived in Zürich, Switzerland's largest city (its capital is Bern). Having written his polemical pamphlets the creative forces were gathering anew: first Wagner wrote the prose outline and libretto for the cycle of *The Ring of the Nibelung*, completed in 1852, then he got going with the musical score for this work. Thus the first three parts, *The Rhine Gold*, *The Valkyrie* and half of *Siegfried*, were wholly completed in 1853-57. He was inspired; for example the score for the first part, *The Rhine Gold*, was done in three months in 1853 according to Mayer. Although it's only a foreplay it still runs for about 2 ½ hours so this was something of a feat.

FORTY

Wagner now was 40 years old. Although in exile and not rich he had food for the day, friends and accommodation and there was a steady growth in interest for his works in France, Germany, and England. These years, 1853-58, Wagner and Minna first spent in the Zürich suburb of Zeltweg. In 1857 the silk merchant Otto Wesendonck invited the pair to live for free in a guest house next to his villa on The Green Hill, Villa Wesendonck, which reportedly still stands.

This seemed fine but an intrigue was brewing. Wagner fell in love with Otto's wife, the musically and poetically gifted Mathilde. The relationship is described as courtly and platonic but it became a scandal nonetheless. Minna wasn't amused and the friendship with Otto soon ended. But the Mathilde-Wagner affair with elements such as forbidden love and indulging in unrelieved feelings had its artistic outlet in the opera *Tristan and Isolde*, which Wagner began working on now. Of course the affair with Mathilde didn't automatically engender this work, Wagner had heard of the story before, but— according to Mayer—Wagner's love for Mathilde was the trigger that made it all into music.

As for triggers in Wagner's creative process Mayer also mentions these: the visit in the Norwegian fjord in 1839 triggered *The Flying Dutchman*, the sight of the castle Wartburg triggered *Tannhäuser*, and a nightly brawl in Nuremberg in 1835 triggered the second finale of *The Master-Singers*. The works in question were mostly the fruits of Wagner's mind but events IRL had the role of catalysts.

- - -

The Wesendonck affair and Wagner's stay in Zürich ended in August 1858. Wagner first moved to Geneva, then to Venice, Italy, where *Tristan* was completed. At the same time he finally divorced Minna.

The pragmatic reason for beginning the *Tristan* work was to have something easily staged to offer opera producers: a one-night show in contrast to the four-night length of The Ring. But even *Tristan* proved hard to sell. A Viennese opera tried to rehearse it but had to give up after 77 attempts; the music and singing were deemed impossible to perform. It was a new kind of work, truly an example of future music, *Zukunftsmusik*, sporting "asymmetrical" chords and wavering tonality. This new kind of music, disharmonic and elusive, was Wagner's way of describing the angst of the pair engaged in their forbidden love affair.

A revised version of *Tannhäuser* was set up in Paris in 1861 but this also became a fiasco. As intimated, the Parisian taste was out of line with Wagner's works. But now, as for Wagner's career, the light came from the east: he was allowed to return to Germany in 1862, he was no longer an exile. First he settled in Biebrich in Prussia.

THE WAGNERIAN PROJECT

As intimated Wagner wasn't active in politics proper after 1849. But emotionally he remained a German nationalist, and set to stage Germanic legends and myths in the form of a music drama. A new opera form was in the making: it had more bass tones and less chirping of the prevalent southern kind, and there was the "endless melody" with no place for separate song numbers. Moreover it was a long work, several hours in duration. This was the Wagnerian style already commenced in *Tannhäuser* and *Lohengrin* and which would be perfected in *The Ring of the Nibelung*, *Tristan and Isolde* and *Parsifal*.

Wagner was something of a nationalist. Then, what's actually "German" in these works and not "human" and "timeless", is a moot point. Wagner's operas today are staged throughout the world and most opera goers appreciate him, his works being part of the opera mainstream. The style is somewhat cosmopolitan. That said, to me it still seems that Wagner had nationalism as a driving force, constantly from returning to Germany in 1842 and on.

As intimated this nationalism at the time was not *comme-il-faut* but revolutionary. Only eventually did Wagner's Germanic heroes and gods, as the world caught up with him, happen to fit the aspirations of the German-Prussian Kaiser State, established in the 1870's. And Wagner played along in this, for example composing a *Kaiser Marsch* and soliciting money for his opera house in Bayreuth from Bismarck.

This might seem like opportunism, a go-with-the-flow nationalism as opposed to Wagner's earlier revolutionary nationalism. And to this criticism I say: Okay. But the origin of this German art form, the impulse to stage music dramas with a sense of northernness, came from Wagner himself, from Wagner as a nationally sensitive poet and composer. I'm not advocating German nationalism or even chauvinism here. For one I'm a Swede, not a German. But as a historian you can't deny that Wagner was driven by ideas of German uniqueness, wishing to elevate his own national characteristics in an art form—opera—in which everything at the time was shaped after southern and antique models.

Wagner of course wasn't totally unique as an artist, creating everything as out of an empty hat. Besides folk tales and myths that he elaborated upon there were precursors such as Goethe, Shakespeare, and (for *The Flying Dutchman*) Henrich Heine. And, as stated earlier, an early inspiration in the opera was Carl Maria von Weber whom the young Wagner had seen in the pulpit at the Dresden opera. von Weber was the man who in 1821 had composed *Der Freischütz*, based on a folk tale about a hunter who enters into a contract with the devil to become a master marksman. This was a "gothic" style which had not previously been seen on the opera stage; there the *Leitkultur* was southern and antique. Weber was the first to include folk music in an operatic work, visualizing the German forest by inserting an instrument such as the French horn. And with his legendary operas Wagner later single-handedly fulfilled this national, gothic, heroic approach in the music theatre.

You must, I think, acknowledge the national profile in Wagner's works, see the passion for his native country and culture in his art. That he also came to denigrate Jewish music (*Das Judenthum in der Musik*, 1869; see chapter 15) is a fact but not of paramount importance, seen on the level of the artistic whole. Wagner, like Ezra Pound, can be seen as having anti-Semitic traits but their respective *oeuvres* aren't anti-Semitic. Correct me if I'm wrong but there are no anti-Semitic *Cantos* and there are no programmatic anti-Semitic Wagner operas. The *Judenthum* pamphlet, as an enterprise, shows us that negativity per se takes you nowhere (the same could be said about Nietzsche's anti-Wagner pamphlet; see chapter 12). Don't be negative and deliberate on what art shouldn't be; this Wagner on the whole may have understood. He liked to be a German, he liked German myths and legends and he put it all on stage in a grand, true fashion. Wagner's familiarity with Germanic myths is what defines his art, what makes him what he is. He wanted to let us hear how a Germanic forest sounds and after *Waldweben* the whole world knows it.

SUCCESS

While living in Biebrich Wagner began work on *The Master Singers of Nuremberg*. This was based on a 1500's historical figure, Hans Sachs and the singer showmanship that used to be a facet of German city life. Like *Rienzi* it was a realistic opera and no fairytale; like *Tristan and Isolde* it was partly written to have something to put on stage without much fuss, a one-night performance and not a four-part cycle like The Ring.

Wagners overall concern by this time was to have The Ring staged at a designated opera house. By this time his dreams in this respect came closer to realization. Because now, in 1864, he was contacted by the newly installed, 18-year-old King Ludwig II of Bavaria. This was to be the crucial breakthrough for Wagner. Ludwig admired Wagner's art and could pay for a few things.

Wagner's first meeting with Ludwig took place in May 1864, in the Bavarian capital Munich. A strange relationship evolved from this. On the one hand we had Ludwig, a art lover, an admirer of bygone times, and sporting traits such as social phobia and homosexuality. He didn't engage in anything improper with Wagner but they often met and rumours of their relationship found its way into the comic magazines of the day. According to Mayer their letters could sound like this, with the king addressing Wagner, "Flamingly beloved! Heavenly friend!", to which Wagner in a more restrained, but fitting manner would write, "Dear, faithful, truly!" The king: "In eternal love and faithfulness to the death, your Ludwig." Wagner: "Eternally your faithful" or "Faithful and loving."

You could say: Wagner just played along. He was dependent on the influence of the king to have his operas performed and his own opera house built. Indeed the friendship with Ludwig was to pave way for a commercial breakthrough for Wagner. Moreover, for Wagner the previous years had been creatively fruitful: more than half of The Ring was completed plus *Tristan* and most of *The Master-Singers*. To this, Mayer, says, Wagner's previous works now were performed in London, Paris, St Petersburg, Moscow, Prague, and Vienna. Sometimes Wagner went himself to these venues to conduct concertos and selections of his work.

The first proof of Ludwig's royal sponsorship was the staging of *Tristan and Isolde* in Munich in 1865. Eventually, thanks to Ludwig's support, the construction of the Festival Hall of Bayreuth was begun. Here Wagner would "realize the idea of a full-fledged performance of the Wagnerian *Gesamtkunstwerk*, in the framework of the *Festspiel* concept".[6]

Wagner eventually settled in Villa Tribschen in Lucerne Switzerland, where he lived 1866-72. In 1868 Wagner also had his first meeting with the philosopher Friedrich Nietzsche, taking place in Germany, and the next year Nietzsche made his first visit to Villa Triebschen. Here, in June 1869, Cosima also bore Wagner the son Siegfried, who later carried on the Wagner heritage in Bayreuth.

In Villa Triebschen Wagner also completed *The Master-Singers of Nuremberg*, which was performed in Munich in 1868. Then it was time for The Ring whose first two parts, on King Ludwig's wish, could be performed in Munich in 1869 and 1870 (*The Rhine Gold* and *The Valkyrie*).

THE RING

As for The Ring it had been left half done for many years. In 1857 Wagner had composed the *Siegfried* score up and until act two; he left off somewhere after Siegfried had killed the dragon. This might seem like a fair place to lay this epic aside for a while, but an almost 15 year hiatus in composing a work is a long time.

---

[6] Jeanson p.91.

The thing of it seems to be this: Wagner was wary of the rest, he had no ideas how he would set music to the plot that he had already outlined. It would prove hard to make the end of a tetralogy work musically. In fact it became something of a mess with leitmotifs stacked upon each other. Wagner had to patch things up. More on this in chapter 10.

However, in 1871 Wagner gathered himself enough to complete the third part of the cycle, *Siegfried*, and in 1874 the last section called *The Twilight of the Gods* was done. He had to stitch and glue and cover up, but in all he pulled it off; although no masterpiece yet the end of The Ring turned out to be feasible. Just before this the theatre in Bayreuth was completed. And here, in this small town in northern Bavaria, the Wagner family finally settled in a house called Villa Wahnfried. It remained in the possession of the Wagner family and became a national shrine à la Goethe's house in Weimar, the so-called German pantheon Walhalla in Bavaria and the *Hermannsdenkmal* in North Rhein-Westphalia. The latter structure, in the form of a statue of Hermann on a high plinth, commemorates the German victory over two Roman legions in Teutoburger Wald, 9 C.E.

Wagner's works thus had a noteworthy success while he lived, his personal triumph coinciding with the outer, political triumph of the German kaiser state with Berlin as capital. Germany's diverse kingdoms and territories were unified under the imperial crown of Vilhelm I, who ruled 1871-1888. Germany was victorious after the decisive, unifying wars of 1866-1871 and wanted to celebrate itself, to which the Germanic music theatre of Wagner was a perfect fit. Wagner for his part didn't rest on his laurels but now wrote his last work, *Parsifal*, which premièred in 1882. Parsifal is really interesting, showing that Wagner still had Christianity on his mind, the opera being about the Grail Knights, the guardians of the chalice with the blood of Christ. He had, for example, planned to do a Jesus Opera once (*Jesus von Nazareth*). Then, during the 1848-49 Revolution, he was more hostile towards Christianity, affected by ideas of materialism of the Feuerbach variety. But Wagner was never an atheist.

In the autumn of the same year, 1882, Wagner began to feel unwell. So he moved with his family to a palace in Venice, Palazzo Vendramin. There he drew his last breath on February 13, 1883, being 69 when he died.

2. THE FAIRIES (1833)

Wagner's first successful opera was *Rienzi*. And I'll get to this and all the other "canonical" works soon. But from early on Wagner wrote many dramas and operas, most of the operas being left half-finished, and it may be interesting to look into them. However, in this chapter I only take a closer look at *The Fairies*, this opera to me symbolizing all the early, promising works of Wagner. In other words, this chapter will be a case of *pars pro toto* (the part standing for the whole). True, in the realm of forgotten, shelved and/or half-finished Wagner operas I also look at *Wieland the Smith* (1850), but that will be in the context where it chronologically belongs.

Now for *The Fairies*. This was Wagner's first completed opera but it was only staged after Wagner's death, the premier taking place in 1888. As a music piece it's of mostly academic interest. Personally I'm rather fascinated by the plot.

COMPOSITION HISTORY

Wagner completed *The Fairies (Die Feen)* in 1833. The opera has three acts. The libretto was written by Wagner, based on a story by Carlo Gozzi called *La donna serpente*. Wagner was only 20 when writing this but he already had some experience from writing, such as the unfinished opera *Die Hochzeit* (1832) and the play *Leubald* (1828).

The word-smith side of opera work came easily to him. In this we also see the worth in completing your works, even though they may seem overly melodramatic like *Leubald*. Even the failed works have something to teach you. The Science Fiction writer Robert Heinlein for his part stressed "finish what you write" as one of the cardinal rules of writing. (For the record his five rules were: 1) write (don't talk about writing) 2) finish what you write 3) send it to a publisher 4) keep sending it 5) don't change anything except on editorial recommendation.)

According to Wikipedia[7] Wagner elaborated a bit on Gozzi's story. For example, the names of the two central characters, Ada and Arindal, are from Wagner's own play *Die Hochzeit*. Also, Wagner's libretto is said to have fantastic traits that we don't find in the original. Wikipedia finally says this about the fate of the original manuscript: Wagner personally gave it to his royal friend Ludwig II of Bavaria. Later the document was given to Adolf Hitler, and as such may have gone up in flames with the fall of Berlin in 1945.

The première of *The Fairies* was given in Munich in 1888, after Wagner's death.

THE PLOT

The plot of *The Fairies* is as follows. During a hunt prince Arindal of Tramond falls into a river and disappears. But he isn't dead; when waking again he finds himself in the castle of a fair damsel. Enamoured he stays with her for eight years.

The woman tells the prince: do not ask my name, do not ask of my heritage, and whatever happens, do not curse me. Happily they live and they have two children. But one day Arindal breaks a part of the promise and is forced to return to his native land, a land in the real world—real even though it's a fictitious land called Tramond. But it's not a land of the fairy world, of elven land, if you follow me; it's in the land of men.

---

[7] Entry: Die Feen.

There, in Tramond, Arindal's father has died. Enemies are occupying the land, having invaded everything but the capital which is defended by Arindal's sister Lora.

The enemy army is led by an Amazon, the self-same woman that Arindal has lived with in fairyland. With her are the two children. In a dramatic scene she hurls them into a burning abyss, also telling everyone that she is Ada, queen of the fairies. Even Arindal doesn't know this name; when they were together he promised not to ask it. The promise he did break must have concerned only her heritage. Now, when the name is out, Arindal breaks the rest of his promise and curses Ada. As a fairy she's immortal, by this time having wished to relinquish her immortality in order to be able to live with Arindal. However, the king of the fairies has forced her to test Arindal's love in this way—because the kids aren't really dead, the hurling act was just an illusion to see if Arindal was steadfast in his love for her.

Now, this is construed into Ada being the one who has failed. She is incarcerated in a stone for a hundred years. Arindal goes nearly mad because of this and runs out to the woods. When out in the wild he meets the sorcerer Groma who gives him a sword, a shield and a lyre with which to win back Ada. Venturing down into the underground Arindal conquers the sentinels guarding the stone in question. And with the lyre the stone is melted. With this proof of his love Arindal is given immortality by the fairy-king, and with Ada he lives happily ever after.

COHERENCE

This a fine story in the realm of fantasy; it's a bit incredible from an everyday point of view but as for being a fairytale, it all makes sense. All the plot elements cohere. Moreover, this was the first of many Wagner dramas on the theme of "love conquers all". Additionally the power of art is beautifully symbolized in the lyre melting the stone. It isn't solely by bravery or cunning the hero succeeds, but also by being able to play and sing. Thus he is something of an Orpheus, the man whose singing even melted the hearts of the gods. Arindal in this respect also mirrors Tannhäuser, the protagonist of another Wagner opera: the singer-cum-poet as a hero.

As stated above Wagner wrote the libretto based on a play by Carlo Gozzi; Lundewall gives us the interesting side-note that Gozzi also wrote the play on which the Puccini opera *Turandot* is based. Lundewall also sees these similarities between *The Fairies* and other Wagner operas: the prohibition to ask the beloved where he/she is from (*Lohengrin*), a woman being punished and held in a dangerous place from which only her lover can rescue her (*The Valkyrie*) and the trying, heroic quest (*Parsifal*). Generally the "redemption through love" —theme seen here is present in almost all Wagner operas. Love conquers all—*amor vincit omnia*.

3. RIENZI, THE LAST OF THE TRIBUNES (1842)

Richard Wagner himself didn't consider *Rienzi* a canonical work of his. Only the works from *Tannhäuser* on were worthy of being called music dramas in the new style, with leitmotifs, the element of "speech-song" and the blotting out of pre-ordained forms such as arias, choruses and duets. However, *Rienzi* has a timeless quality to it and has been performed widely ever since Wagner's death.

ORIGINS

Rienzi, the Last of the Roman Tribunes (1835) is a novel written by British author Edward Bulwer-Lytton (1803-1873). Somehow Richard Wagner got hold of a copy of this story of a medieval Italian soldier becoming a populist ruler of Rome.

According to Klas Ralf (libretto to *The Flying Dutchman*, 1977), in the spring of 1838 Wagner, living in Riga, was working on a libretto to *Rienzi*. According to other sources Wagner had completed about two acts of the opera when he left Riga and arrived in London in 1839. By then it was August. Wagner, Lundewall says, had wanted to meet up with Bulwer-Lytton and show him the libretto but the author wasn't in town.

Wagner and Minna soon continued to Paris, France, the cultural capital of Europe. Wagner by this time was occupied with other projects too—magazine articles, smaller musical works —but his main effort seems to have been to complete *Rienzi*. He began composing the score in 1839 and it was finished in November, 1840. With the help of the composer Meyerbeer, *Rienzi* was soon accepted by the Dresden Opera. It premièred on October 20, 1842 and was something of a success.

MELODRAMA

Rienzi is a heroic opera with a political theme. The events have historical foundation; however the plot is based on Bulwer-Lytton's novel, and as such it gets a little melodramatic. Still, it's rather unique for an opera to have political issues at the centre of the plot, at least intimating such issues as democracy, tyranny, aristocratic republicanism, and the political role of the church. The scene is 14th century Rome, by then a very small state, one of many Italian principalities, colonies, lands and dominions, but precisely by it being a small state, the action becomes eminently concentrated, making each participating faction—the aristocracy, the church, the people and The Man of Action—into a telling symbol, echoing other men of action and factions throughout history, having battled for power in the setting of a capital.

As for stage acts, the best work to compare Wagner's *Rienzi* with is Shakespeare's *Julius Caesar*. It has the same concentration, and the same way of transforming political issues into a relatable narrative.

The historical Cola di Rienzi is said to have lived 1313-1354. He was called "the last of the tribunes"; in ancient, Republican Rome B.C. tribunes acted as a sort of *ombudsmen* for the people against the aristocracy. And in medieval Rome Rienzi played this role, reviving the institution and thus echoing ancient times. Supported by the people, Rienzi came to power but in the end everything turned against him, even popular opinion.

This opera has a magnificent overture. The trumpet call at the beginning is both ominous and triumphant, being the war call of the

Colonna family. Then it evolves into a symphonic poem of alluring beauty, pompous and grand but also romantic and sweeping. Finally it ends as a military march: more pomp and circumstance, but it blends in well. Even though Wagner himself wasn't so delighted with *Rienzi* this overture is still a substantial piece. There's nothing "immature", "early" or "undeveloped" about it. It's just great—great as a Wagner piece, showing all that is both excellent and questionable with the Wagner style. It's over the top, pompous, elaborate and melodic at the same time.

In short: if you like Wagner you'll like the Rienzi overture. And conversely: if you're not attracted by the Rienzi overture there's the possibility that you won't like the rest of Wagner's *oeuvre* either.

POWER STRUGGLE

In the beginning of the opera Rienzi emerges as a man of the people, an alternative to the warring factions of aristocrats. The people present him with the crown of Rome but he refuses it, only wishing to be a People's Tribune. This is reminiscent of the first act of Shakespeare's *Julius Caesar*, when the hero of the play abstains from being crowned with the diadem, the traditional Roman royal attribute.

By this Rienzi becomes Rome's ruler, without any fighting or bloodshed. The aristocrats simply flee, abandoning the political centre stage in face of this populist upsurge. However, in the following act the aristocrats plan to murder Rienzi. But it comes to nothing more than an attempt. Next the aristocracy marches on Rome with an army; this gives Rienzi the opportunity to really be the leader of the people, rousing them to defend their city and defeat the nobles. The nobles then get support from notable powers such as the Pope and the Emperor of Germany. Both these powers exerted hegemony over Italy at the time, the former spiritually, the latter in a more hands-on fashion. The Pope lays a papal ban on Rienzi threatening to excommunicate him, literally kick him out of the church, which in these times was a punishment worse than death, a symbolical shutting out of a man from the society of men and God. But Rienzi's faith is asserted in his prayer, the song "Allmächt'ger Vater, blickt herab" ("Almighty Father, Look Down").

Rienzi is becoming isolated in his Capitol dwelling; in Act 3 he only has his sister Irene with him. She is courted by the aristocrat Adriano who now wishes her to come with him and leave her brother. But Irene stays on, even when Rienzi realizes that his game is coming to an end; for example, he gets to know that his enemies are planning to burn the Capitol, his palace on the Capitoline Hill. And when he tries to speak to the people the crowd turns against him. Then everything literally goes down in flames, the Capitol collapses and Rienzi and Irene are killed in the commotion.

This might seem very melodramatic. All I can say about that is: true! The historical Rienzi didn't end his days like that. But to stage a story you sometimes need to condense elements of it. Again, compare this with Shakespeare who also told us violent, sometimes "incredible" stories. As for melodrama, this Rienzi story might also have affected latter-day filmmakers. At least I would like to parallel the end of it with the final part of Brian De Palma's *Scarface* (1983). There, in a contemporary American setting, we also have a southern gentleman meeting the fall of his empire in his castle, accompanied by his sister. Now Scarface had a more complicated relationship with his sister than Rienzi, but in general I'd say that both *Rienzi* and *Scarface* are classic stories, dense plots showing the rise and fall of an outsider.

POPULIST RULER

Bulwer-Lytton telescoped the Rienzi narrative into a tragedy, making it relatable for the common man. And Wagner put it all upon the stage: the outsider comes to town, starts a new regime but in the end is overcome by mighty forces. In real life Rienzi didn't die in a burning Capitolium, but he did challenge the Powers that Be.

According to Wikipedia[8] Rienzi challenged the Pope and the Emperor with his vision of a new empire, based on the will of the people. Then Martin Luther did the same. And Napoleon. And, in a way, Hitler. Small wonder then that the latter was affected by seeing this opera in Linz at the beginning of the 20th century, an experience which is said to have served as a catalyst for the whole of Hitler's political project. More on this in chapter 15.

---

[8] Entry: Cola di Rienzo.

4. THE FLYING DUTCHMAN (1843)

The Flying Dutchman is the next oldest of Wagner's operas that is still played in opera houses around the world. The oldest is *Rienzi*. Scholars point to these operas and say that they're a bit primitive, having got separate numbers like arias, duets and choruses. But in essence there's nothing primitive about them. To what degree Wagner's earlier works are different from his canonical works is something for academics to discuss. *The Flying Dutchman* for its part is fresh and vital, with the atmosphere of the sea, the seaman's life and shipping blowing at you in every song.

BACKGROUND

In 1977 the royal Swedish opera, *Kungliga Teatern,* staged *The Flying Dutchman.* In conjunction with that they issued the libretto with German and Swedish text. In an appendix Klas Ralf wrote about the origins of the drama.

Thus it was: Wagner, living in Riga 1838 as a conductor at Deutsches Teater, in the spring of that year read a story about the legendary Flying Dutchman, a story printed in 1830. Later in 1838 Wagner, according to Ralf, read Heinrich Heine's story on the same subject, "Memoiren des Herren von Schnabelewopski". Heine's version was a vaguely satirical take on this myth of the sea captain doomed to sail the seas forever.

Wagner is said to have performed well as a maestro in Riga but for some reason the direction didn't like him. At the same time the Wagners had been living above their means so Wagner and Minna decided to flee Riga in July 1839, planning to go to London then Paris. And on July 19 they boarded the sailing ship Thetis in Pillau, East Prussia. By July 27-29 they endured a storm in Skagerack, having to seek refuge in Sandvika on the island of Boröya, outside of Arendal on the Norwegian south coast. Staying in Sandvika for a few days Wagner heard the shouts of the sailors, which are said to have found their way into the "Chorus of the Norwegian Sailors" in the beginning of Act 3 of the eventually completed opera.

Thetis and the Wagners finally arrived in London on August 12, having endured another storm on the North Sea. These maritime adventures, and the reading of Heine's story, influenced Wagner into making The Dutchman story into an opera. At this time he was occupied with composing *Rienzi* but in 1840, in Paris, he met Heine himself who approved of his plans to base an opera libretto on his, Heine's, short story. Some time later Wagner wrote a prose outline for the opera, giving it to the Grand Opéra in Paris in the summer of 1840 in the hope that they would assign him the task of composing an opera to it. At the same time he started composing parts of it, like "Senta's Ballade" and "Chorus of the Norwegian Sailors". This was at the end of July according to Ralf.

The autumn was spent in completing the *Rienzi* libretto. Then, in May 1841, Wagner made a first draft of a German libretto to *The Dutchman*. In June, having learned that *Rienzi* would be staged in Dresden, he started composing the music to *The Dutchman*. At the same time the Paris opera had bought his French outline for the opera; however, they assigned the writing of the libretto and the music to some Frenchmen, staging it as *Le Vaisseau fantôme* in 1842. It made little impression.

Before this, in the summer of 1841, Wagner completed most of the score to *The Dutchman*. In November he composed the overture and then it was done. Next year, in April, the Wagners left France for Germany and Dresden, for the première of *Rienzi*. In the wake of this success Wagner also got *The Dutchman* accepted at the Dresden opera. It premièred in January 1843 with Wagner himself as conductor. It was moderately well received but there were only four shows in all. Ralf concludes that this opera musically was ahead of its time.

A SYMBOL OF THE ARTIST

The legend of The Flying Dutchman is old, this story about a sea captain cursing God during a storm. Trying to round the Cape of Good Hope he says that he'd rather sail the seas until doomsday than give up his attempt. Having put himself up against God in this way he becomes "the Wandering Jew of the oceans", finding rest nowhere. Wagner got his plot mainly from Heine's short story, where we see the Dutchman being redeemed by the love of a faithful woman. As I said Heine's story was somewhat ironic, but Wagner took it seriously. And why not: it is artistic freedom as they call it.

However, you must admit that the story lends itself to an ironic version too. Overall it's a many-faceted story with some inner truth to it. The sailor doomed to sail the seas forever is like Ahashverus, the Jew doomed to wander the earth after having mocked Jesus on the cross. Also, the restless spirit of the Dutchman can be seen as a symbol of the ambitious artist, always out there in order to create the next big work. He can make port sometimes, he can meet ordinary people and even have his amorous encounters, but in essence these are just intermezzos, his real life being to sail The Seas of Fate trying to reach the unreachable.

SANDVIK

As any other Wagner opera *The Flying Dutchman* has three acts. In Act 1 the immediate background is this: the merchant mariner Daland is on his way home, sailing for Norway. He can almost spot his home-port. However, a storm forces him to seek refuge in a bay called Sandvik (Sandy Bay). The action begins with the ship having cast anchor, waiting out the foul weather. Going ashore Daland muses about the storm and how near to home they are, only seven miles. And soon, he feels, they can set sail again for the last leg of the trip. Soon they shall meet their beloved ones waiting at home.

Daland and his crew go to rest. Only a helmsman keeps guard and he soon falls asleep. Then the stage directions tell us about the storm still raging and a ship approaching, with black masts and red sails: the ship of The Flying Dutchman. Eventually it anchors in the bay next to Daland's ship. The ghostly crew takes down the sails and the Dutchman steps ashore, wearing a black Spanish outfit and sporting a black beard.

Scene two opens with The Dutchman singing an aria, usually named by its first line, "Die Frist is um" (The Respite Has Come), telling us of his condition: being doomed to sail the seas forever he can be redeemed if he during a regular seven year respite finds a woman that loves him. But he is despondent, seemingly doomed to live forever as a sea-farer:

Nirgends ein Grab! Niemals der Tod!
Dies der Verdamnis Schreckgebot.[9]

Freely translated: "Nowhere a grave! Never dead! / That's my cruel punishment."

DALAND

Scene three. Daland, exiting his cabin, looks around and spots the anchored ship of The Dutchman. With his helmsman he calls the ship but no one answers. The helmsman shouts again: *Gebt Antwort! Schiff und Flagge?* (Answer! Ship and flag?) This may be a fairytale but in details such as these an atmosphere of authenticity is created. It's like Poe at his best: everyday details co-existing with the grotesque and the arabesque.

---

[9] The Flying Dutchman, p.3.

Then Daland sees The Dutchman ashore and calls him, asking him who he is. The Dutchman answers:

Weit komm ich her: verwehrt bei Sturm und Wetter
ihr mir den Ankerplatz?[10]

Freely translated: "Long was my way: will you, by storm and tempest, / refuse me the anchorage?" Daland says he won't, "hospitality lives in Norway. Who are you?" "Dutchman," comes the succinct answer.

They strike up a conversation. A strange man the Dutchman is but at the same time he's rich. And when The Dutchman learns that Daland has a daughter he wants her for his bride. Daland quickly agrees to this; a son in law rich in jewels and gold, what more can you ask for? At the same time the northerly storm has given way for a southern breeze, enabling Daland to sail home. The Dutchman promises that he will follow suit.

SENTA

This opera plays in Norway which Wagner, as we saw, had visited once: like the sailors in Act 1 he had to seek refuge in a Norwegian port after a storm, when he and Minna sailed from Riga to London in 1839. The songs of the sailors and other maritime elements of that trip are said to have influenced the opera in question. And the name of the heroine, Senta, according to an ad-note to the libretto issued by Kungliga Teatern 1977, is created by Wagner on this ground: the Norwegian word for girl is *jente,* older form *jenta*. This word, you could surmise, was heard by Wagner during his Norwegian intermezzo, and to make it pronounceable in German he made the heroine's name into *Senta,* resulting in a unique, fairy-talish name.

Senta is Daland's daughter. In Act 2 we meet her in her parent's home where she sits staring at a picture of The Dutchman. She knows of his plight, of having to sail the seas forever unless he can

---

[10] Ibid p.4.

find a woman who loves him. All is said in the musical highlight of this opera, "Senta's Ballad", an operatic aria with folk-song qualities. *Johohoe! Johohe! Hui!* It's like nothing I've heard before, dramatic and gripping, not exactly emotionally gripping but captivating and alluring in an indescribable manner. That's how it is with Wagner operas: when reading the libretti they may seem a bit contrived but when listening to the music it envelops and raises the narrative to a higher level.

Next Senta meets with her present lover, the hunter Erik. He has seen how she sits in trance before the picture of The Dutchman but now, asked by Erik about this habit, she belittles it. However, soon she is drawn to the picture again, empathizing with the doomed man. Erik then tells her of a vision he has had, one of Senta meeting with The Dutchman and sailing away with him. Senta absent-mindedly seems pleased to hear this and by this Erik has had enough, leaving abruptly.

Seamlessly this transfers into the next scene, with Daland entering the house accompanied by the Dutchman. Of course Senta and The Dutchman fall in love. After an introductory aria Daland leaves the two. The pair then sings a duet in which Senta says she will share his misery. It's "redemption through love", "impossible love" and all the other elements of Wagnerian romance. When Daland returns Senta says that she will marry The Dutchman and love him through thick and thin.

FINALE

The final act begins with a famous Wagner chorus, "Chorus of the Norwegian Sailors". In the port of the unnamed Norwegian city where the action takes place the sailors of Daland's ship sing a song of the invigorating life at sea. It's very apt, like most of this opera catching the spirit of the sea. Somewhat later we get a juxtaposition of this hearty song in the form of "The Ghost Chorus", sung by the crew of The Dutchman's ship. Actually, this isn't so scary or ghostlike. It's dramatic, being a repetition of the first part of the overture, but that chilling character you might expect from a ghost choir just isn't there. Only later in his career Wagner got the hang of ambiguous, grey-area, otherworldly tones, like the latter parts of The Ring or *Tristan* with their tendencies to atonality, half-tones and angst.

In the last scene Senta and Erik meet outside Senta's house. Erik tries to draw her out of the spell of The Dutchman. For instance, in a song (labelled *cavatina*—"short song") he reminds her of how once they came to be a pair, with Daland having entrusted her in his care. The charming scene painted by this song, overheard by The Dutchman, makes him cry out that he is lost. The pair spots him and Senta begs him to stay. But no, he now has to go to sea again, sailing forever like a moron. Why The Dutchman can't listen to Senta's pledges of love is a bit hard to understand. The answer seems to be: she didn't swear him eternal love in the presence of God, only to him. This seems contrived in order to "tragedize" the plot at the finale.

The Dutchman shows her his fearful ship: you surely don't want to sail on this? And so he gets aboard and sails away. But Senta, held by Erik and Daland, breaks loose, runs up a cliff and throws herself into the ocean, singing:

Preis deinen Engel und sein Gebot!
Hier steh' ich treu dir bis zum Tod![11]

Freely translated: "Praise your angel and its command! / Here I stand, faithful to the end!"

Opera producers staging *The Flying Dutchman* sometimes let the opera end by this. By convention it's deemed okay to skip some of the stage directions if you feel like it, indeed, even to strike out passages of the libretto proper. Letting this opera end by Senta throwing herself into the sea has a distinct tragic quality about it, with everything ending in death, doom and despair. But there are more directions to be had, and in Wagner's vision in the libretto this is how it all ends after Senta has taken a dip: the ship of The Dutchman sinks

---

[11] Ibid p.23.

with men and all. The sea rises and then sinks in a maelstrom. In the rays of the rising sun we see, over the wreckage, the transfigured shapes of Senta and The Dutchman embracing each other, rising over the water's surface and soaring upwards.

That's the whole end but this can seem a bit too sugary and adapted to bourgeois tastes. The nature of fairytale is often harsh and unrelenting and the abrupt death of Senta and the ship of The Dutchman just sailing away is more in spirit with the fairytale, I figure.

5. TANNHÄUSER (1845)

The opera *Tannhäuser* premièred in 1845, classified as a middle-period Wagner opera along with *Lohengrin* (1850). The early period in this respect was *Rienzi* and *The Dutchman*, the late period being The Ring, *Tristan and Isolde* and *Parsifal*. *Tannhäuser* is about an artist being torn between "sacred and profane love", all in a fantasy and medieval setting.

ORIGINS

Tannhäuser has two roots: fairytale and history. As for the tale of the grotto of Venus, Wagner is said (by Wikipedia) to have received it from a Heinrich Heine poem, "Elementargeister" ("Elementals"). Other sagas also may also have inspired the plot, and as for history Wagner was allured by stories about medieval German poets, wandering minstrels. Tannhäuser is a historical figure but rather little is known of him. Wagner in this opera was original in combining reality with myth, in telling about a human being in 14th century Germany that both for a while lives with the love goddess and takes part in the kind of singers' contests that were a craze in those times.

Wagner mainly wrote *Tannhäuser* while he was working as a conductor in Dresden. The prose draft to the opera was written in the summer of 1842. The libretto was written in 1843. The score was completed in April 1845. Finally, the première was given in the Royal Theatre in Dresden on October 19, 1845.

RICHARD WAGNER — A PORTRAIT

POETIC HERO

Plot wise *Tannhäuser* is interesting in that the hero is a poet. To compare with films they seldom succeed in portraying authors. The unique character of being an author/poet etc. doesn't translate well onto the screen. I know, there are some author heroes on the screen but it's much easier to portray "any other profession", I would think.

Now, Tannäuser being a medieval poet also means that he was a singer. This, the performing side of it, is more stage friendly than being a modern poet who primarily sits at home writing books. And as for movies about singers there are many appropriate ones, catching the spirit of being a performing artist, like biopics about Elvis, Buddy Holly, Johnny Cash, Edith Piaf etc.

In medieval times the main heroic archetype was *the knight*. Tannhäuser may have been some kind of nobleman too but it's the poet role that sets him apart. Moreover this is a fairytale swinging between the extremes of happy-go-easy, recreational love and the love that lasts forever, symbolized by the women figures of Venus and Elisabeth respectively, with Tannhäuser thus being torn between a noble virgin and the love goddess herself. It's about grand emotions, the opus by Jeanson said to be "a reflection of Wagner's own, hysterically unbalanced nature, oscillating between eros and Ethos, Wagner himself describing his nature as 'nie und nirgends etwas nur ein wenig, sondern alles voll und ganz' (never and nowhere just a little, but everything to the fullest)".[12] The plot: the wandering minstrel Tannhäuser has been living with Venus, the goddess of love, for seven years. Having an inkling that this is a life in sin he invokes the Virgin Mary seven times. Thus he again ends up in the everyday world, in a valley in Thuringia, a German state situated north of Bavaria and east of Saxony.

Next the action moves to a castle, Wartburg, where Tannhäuser is invited to stay. Tannhäuser falls in love with its ruler, princess Elisabeth. Together with other minstrels, poets and singers Tannhäuser enters a singing contest on the Wartburg premises. In

---

[12] Jeanson p.74; translated by the author.

his entry Tannhäuser praises the goddess of love, which is seen as a blasphemy. He is sentenced to seek grace and expiation from his deed at the papal seat in Rome.

A year later Tannhäuser returns to Wartburg. He says to his friends that the Pope has turned him down and sentenced him to eternal damnation. Therefore he plans to return to Venus, since it is as impossible for him to be redeemed as it is for the papal staff to blossom.

At this very moment a train of mourners arrive, carrying the dead Elisabeth. Full of remorse Tannhäuser sinks to the ground and dies. Then some pilgrims arrive, carrying the blossoming staff of the Pope, acknowledging that Tannhäuser is saved.

The plot as whole is feasible, as a fairytale working with symbols. I mean, within the framework of Christian thought the idea of the Pope turning down a repentant sinner is unrealistic. But this plot element is needed in order for the ending to be even more dramatic, giving us the telling symbol of the blossoming staff as a symbolic gesture of redemption. Not that I endorse the idea of "being damned" and then "redeemed", not by outer forces, but within the framework of Christianity it all eventually makes sense. Wagner in *Tannhäuser* condenses the ideas of love, lust and spiritual love into a tight but loose narrative.

THE MUSIC

Musically *Tannhäuser* was innovative with the first consistent use of the Wagnerian "speech song", making the music run through the entire opera without interruption for specific numbers such as arias, duets, chorals etc., as we had seen in *Rienzi* and *The Dutchman*. In addition, Wagner used *leitmotifs* (guiding phrases), a term not created by him, but which describes the kind of musical signatures he weaves into the work, presenting different characters and moods. Later, for example, the Siegfried theme and the Tristan chord became famous leitmotifs in the Wagnerian *oeuvre*. More on leitmotifs in chapter 17.

6. LOHENGRIN (1850)

The opera *Lohengrin* premièred in 1850. It's a traditional yet timeless tale, never going out of fashion. It's a fairytale and legend but as such a succinct story, easier to grip than the same director's *The Ring of the Nibelung*. The Ring of course has its charm, having with its three full-length operas plus a prologue true epic width. *Lohengrin* is a bit more stringent, overall making more sense.

ARTHURIAN LEGEND

In the legends of Arthurian knights we, among others, meet Parsifal and his son, Lohengrin. Parsifal was later to become another Wagner opera. Wagner is said to have read about Lohengrin in Wolfram von Eschenbach's epic poem *Parzival*, in *Der Schwanen-Ritter* by Konrad von Würzburg and in *Das Nibelungenlied*.

Wagner wrote the libretto and score of his Lohengrin opera from September 1846 through April 1848. Then the revolution hit Dresden where Wagner lived, and a year later Wagner had to flee Dresden and Germany and seek refuge in Switzerland. However, at the behest of his friend Franz Liszt *Lohengrin* was staged in Weimar in Thuringia. This 1850 première sported a rather small orchestra (consisting of 38 musicians instead of the usual 105) so this show wasn't altogether convincing. In 1858 Munich a more full-fledged production was staged, sponsored by the Wagner adorer king Ludwig II.

SYNOPSIS

Hereby a synopsis of *Lohengrin*, its main action and what this make me think of.

The story takes place in the duchy of Brabant, a medieval state situated in today's Netherlands. The queen, Elsa of Brabant, has been accused of witchcraft: once she went out in the woods with her brother but he, for his part, never returned. This, her enemies say, is due to her dabblings in the black arts. She now wants to stage a duel to find out the truth: "submit to God's judgment through ordeal by combat" as Wikipedia states.[13] One of the fighters is Telramund, the one who has delivered the accusation and wants to be the ruler of Brabant. Elsa's champion will be someone she has seen in her dreams:

In lichter Waffen Scheine
ein Ritter nahte da,
so tugendlicher Reine
ich keinen noch ersah:
ein golden Horn zur Hüften,
gelehnet auf sein Schwert –
so trat er aus den Lüften
zu mir, der Recke wert...[14]

Freely translated: "In the lustre of bright weapons / a knight approached me, / so virtuous and pure / like no one on earth: / a golden horn at his hip, / leaning on his sword – / thus he, the worthy knight, / out of the blue came to me."

Elsa wants this man as her champion. The king of Germany, Heinrich, lets his herald announce that anyone who wants to fight for Elsa should come forth. The stage is set and truly, a knight soon arrives at the scene. It's an entrance to remember: the man comes over the nearby river, standing in a shell drawn by a swan... This is originally a classic folk tale so Wagner himself hasn't created this

---

[13] Entry: Lohengrin (Wagner).
[14] Lohengrin, p.4.

vision. And perhaps this is on the border between the sublime and the ridiculous, especially when it's presented on a stage. But it's said: opera scenography will always be a problematic art form. It will never look natural, whatever you do. You can also say: everything you present on stage becomes symbolical, even a kitchen sink. As a librettist and scenographer you'll have to accept this, yea, even embrace it, choosing elements that work symbolically. As a dramatist you sometimes have to go the narrow *Sirat bridge* between the sublime and ridiculous. Otherwise you achieve nothing.

In his stage directions Wagner says that the knight is dressed in silvery armour, shield slung on his back, a golden horn at his side and armed with a sword. This is the model "knight in shining armour" and the forte of this play is that it takes the legend seriously. A knight fighting not for money or gold but in order to protect the innocent.

The knight arriving on the cochlea is called Lohengrin. But this we don't get to know yet. He's just a stranger, a heroic champion seemingly from nowhere. He now says he wants to fight for Elsa. He also wants to marry her, on the condition that she never asks about his name. This is a known element of fairytale all over the world: a dream husband or wife who agrees to marriage on the condition of "no questions asked". No inquiries are to be made about the origins of this supernatural person. In the end, the question is posed anyway and the magic is broken, the fairy person has to go. For example this theme can be found in a Japanese tale about a snow queen. And in Wagner's own *The Fairies*, see chapter 2.

Back to *Lohengrin*. Next, the duel is fought. Lohengrin wins. This is in the opera's Act 1. Act 2 develops Elsa's faithfulness to Lohengrin and Telramund's and his sister Ortrud's ulterior motives.

BRIDAL CHORUS

In the beginning of Act 3 Elsa and Lohengrin marries. This is accompanied by "The Bridal Chorus", known by anyone who has seen a wedding if only on film or television. The words that go with it begin by:

> *Treulich geführt ziehet dahin,*
> *wo euch der Segen der Liebe bewahr'!*
> *Siegreicher Mut, Minnegewinn*
> *eint euch in Treue zum seligsten Paar.*[15]

Freely translated: "Faithfully led venture inside, / glorious passion guarding you there! / Victory, joy, courteous love / unite you forever in holiest bond."

An exciting scene is when Telramund breaks into the pair during the wedding night, trying to kill Lohengrin. The result is that the attacker draws the short straw: Telramund is killed by Lohengrin. But this is merely one aspect of this denouement; right before, Elsa has asked Lohengrin his name and where he is from. Lohengrin, telling the courtiers to carry off the dead body, announces that he will tell them all about himself the next day, before the king.

MONSALVAT

In order to keep their strength in fighting for Good the Grail knights must remain anonymous, not telling where they are from. This is a viable attitude, symbolizing the idea of the strong not being driven by hopes of fame and renown, fighting for ideals being its own reward. Therefore, keep a low profile and don't shout out your name at every street-corner. But now, as Elsa already has asked the forbidden questions Lohengrin has to tell them everything, beginning:

> *In fernem Land, unnahbar euren Schritten,*
> *liegt eine Burg, die Monsalvat gennant;*
> *ein lichter Tempel stehet dort inmitten,*
> *so kostbar, als auf Erden nichts bekannt…*[16]

---

[15] Ibid p.25.
[16] Ibid p.32.

Freely translated: "In a faraway land, unreachable by you / is a castle called Monsalvat; / a lovely temple is in the midst of it, / as dear as nothing on earth."

Next Lohengrin tells of the chalice, the knights who guard it and the vows to fight anonymously. Then he says: my father is Parsifal and my name is Lohengrin. And in spite of protests he must return: *Schon zürnt der Gral, dass ich ihm ferne bleib'!* ("Already the Grail is angry that I haven't returned!").

Lohengrin must leave. But at the same time it's revealed that the sister of Telramund, Ortrud, is the one who has been doing the witchcraft, that which Elsa was accused of. Now it's revealed that Ortrud turned Elsa's brother into a swan; also, this was the swan which drew Lohengrin's shell when he arrived. The brother is now re-charmed and comes back to life as a human being. By the way, the Ortrud figure is said to be Wagner's own invention, thus being a proof of his story telling abilities. Having Ortrud as another malignant force besides Telramund gives the plot more direction.

Last, Lohengrin leaves on his shell, this time pulled by a dove from heaven, a Christian element; the Holy Spirit as a dove occurs in several gospels. At the sight of this departure Elsa falls down dead in her brother's arms, a real "operatic end", again sublime bordering on the ridiculous. But again, to portray a story like this on a stage you have to condense it into symbolic gestures.

Otherwise *Lohengrin* as intimated is a moderate length opera, well proportioned. It's a manageable story ended in a one evening show, not spread out over four evenings like The Ring. And unlike that one we find in *Lohengrin* no gods on stage: to portray human beings credibly is one thing while to capture the essence of gods on stage is difficult, to say the least. In tales by modern authors the gods always tend to be humanized and pulled down into the dirt.

Therefore, among other things, it might be more difficult for modernist directors to destroy *Lohengrin* than it is to destroy The Ring. Not that they haven't tried...! Furthermore, what makes *Lohengrin* work on stage is that it's a genuine fairytale, a Nordic-Germanic tale without too many patched-on Christian elements as the same composer's *Tannhäuser*. For instance, in the latter drama they pray to God and everything magically comes true, like the Pope's staff blooming. In the previous chapter I thought this was okay from a Christian point of view. But this could also be seen as a primitive world view, one that isn't genuinely Christian. *Lohengrin,* however, is a more full-fledged fairytale where the simplicity of the symbolism speaks with more credibility: a noble knight shows up and rescues a victim, then he disappears when the oath not to ask about his origins is broken. On the way he has fought evil in the form of an usurper who believes that the end justifies the means.

In other words *Lohengrin* works on its premises. In the context of a fairytale it's consistent and logical. The basic story isn't ruined with too much recent additions, such as Christian moral. It's a timeless story that is well fit to be reproduced as musical theatre, film and novel.

THE MUSIC OF LOHENGRIN

My favourite piece from Lohengrin is "Prelude to the Third Act", shooting off with verve and zest, a brilliant orchestral piece to hum along with. This is a symphonic poem of the lighter, but not sweetish or overly snug kind. Wagner indeed sometimes resorted to this style, the syrupy and cosy. You can say: his musical kernel is melodic, wide and true but he can tend to overproduction and decoration.

In this Wagner opera I also like the bridal chorus, being along with Mendelsohn's wedding march the most common marriage music. When the bride goes up to the altar, led by his father, they often choose "Bridal Chorus from Lohengrin". It is Wagner's most famous work. "Everyone" has heard it. I get the impression that this piece is default choice in Anglo-American realms whereas we in northern Europe have Mendelsohn's song as the most chosen wedding song.

7. WIELAND THE SMITH (1850)

In 1849-1850 Wagner wrote a prose draft for an opera, *Wieland the Smith* (*Wieland der Schmied*). According to Wikipedia it has later on, after Wagner's death, been given a musical score. As such it was performed in Bratislava in 1926. However, in this chapter the focus is on the story itself.

Wieland the Smith is interesting in that it takes an old Nordic myth and treats it with sincerity. Wagner had a predilection for these stories; apart from the traditional side he maybe saw something of himself in them. For instance, in *Wieland the Smith* we have the element of a dead swan and this we also see in *Parsifal* and *Lohengrin*. The elements of a spear and a wound are also seen in *Parsifal*. The elements of a ring and of smithy are seen in The Ring, the forbidden question is seen in *The Fairies* and *Lohengrin* and the element of a dead father could be traced to Wagner's own childhood with his father Friedrich dying early.

Wieland the Smith is based on a story found in The Poetic Edda and later elaborated in medieval Nordic stories. The plot: a young princess meets a prince in the shape of a swan. He says he wants to marry her on the condition that she never asks where he's from. She agrees to this. Then, by the magic power of love, he assumes human shape. They marry, they have children and all is well. But of course she eventually has to ask the forbidden question. Then the prince is transformed into a swan once more; he flies away and the princess is alone with their three daughters.

The daughters also have the ability to shape-shift into swans. This comes in handy when their kingdom is threatened by the invasion of an enemy tribe, the Nidungs. The girls are given the orders by their mother to fly away and warn the land of the invasion. While flying one of the three, Svanhilde, is hit by a spear and falls to the earth. But the backwoods smith Wieland rescues her. Having fallen in love with him, Svanhilde renounces her half-divine nature by taking off a magic ring her mother gave her. She also takes off her swan suit.

One day while Wieland is out on an errand the countess Bathilde approaches their hut in the woods. Bathilde steals the magic ring, has Svanhilde brought along and the hut burned down. Wieland, on returning having seen his world been shattered to pieces, goes out on a quest to find his wife. Eventually he ends up at Bathilde's court. There he is charmed by the powers of her ring and is imprisoned, forced to make weapons for the countess.

After some cumbersome happenings Wieland remembers Svanhilde and his promise to find her and avenge her. Now Bathilde is in love with Wieland. Also, he is crippled by having his Achilles tendons cut off, to hinder him from escaping. In the end the Nidungs arrive threatening them all, but Wieland being the handyman he is has made himself a couple of wings with which he can take to the air. While in flight he attacks Bathilde's castle with fire, burning it to the ground with all its inhabitants. Still in flight he hears the sound of Svanhilde crying out; he rescues her and flies away with her.

I don't know what to make of this. I only know that the Wieland/Valand character through the years has fascinated two Swedish authors. First, Viktor Rydberg (1828-1895) focuses rather a lot on the elves Ivalde with sons Slagfinn, Egil and Valand in his outline of Nordic mythology, *Our Fathers' Godsaga* (*Fädrens gudasaga*, 1887). For instance, Rydberg stresses that these fellows weren't dwarfs, as some say they were, but elves. In early times the elves were companions of the Aesir and Valand fashioned divine artefacts such as Odin's spear Gungner, Frey's ship Skidbladner and Siv's golden hair. This story from Snorre's Edda Rydberg relates in some detail, the story of how the elven smiths compete with the underground smiths

(Dain, Dvalin etc.). The latter win this competition, their gifts (like Thor's hammer) deemed better than Valand's creations.

So it goes. And later, in relating the Snorre story of Odin, Höner and Loki meeting the eagle Tjatse (originally found at the beginning of *Skáldskaparmál* of Snorre's Edda), Rydberg tells us that this eagle was Valand in animal form. Many such ingenious interpretations, with or without elves in the roles, we find in *Our Fathers' Godsaga*.

Another Swedish author, Åke Ohlmarks (1911-1984), for his part classifies Valand as a dwarf. Apart from that, in his *Sagan om Nibelungarna* (1973) he connects the Valand narrative with the Rhine Gold, Sigurd Fafnesbane and all. The Wagnerian mood is vaguely present in this; however, Ohlmarks has made a more or less original take on the whole. "There is more than one way to skin a cat" they say, and there is more than one way for a modern author to elaborate and/or retell the Nordic myths and legends. The gaps in the stories invite you to fill in, recombine and reforge it all into this or the other narrative structure.

8. TRISTAN AND ISOLDE (1865)

Tristan and Isolde is an opera about love, forbidden love. The pair can't be together. But in the central scene of the central act they meet and indulge in this forbidden game, all expressed in a harrowing, angst-ridden score. At the time of the première it was called *Zukunftsmusik*—"The Music of the Future". This was something of a put-down then. But now we know that the Tristan music has stood the test of time.

BACKGROUND

As related in chapter 1 Wagner had to flee from Dresden in May, 1849, having to give up his position as a conductor, his home and everything. He was a revolutionary with a warrant posted for his arrest, having taken part in the unsuccessful May revolution. His wife Minna was left in Dresden for a while but Wagner eventually came to Switzerland where he was given a place to stay at the wealthy silk trader Otto Wesendonck's estate in Zürich. Wagner's love for Otto's wife Mathilde spurred some of the composing of Tristan, being as it is a medieval tale of forbidden love.

According to Wikipedia[17] Wagner read about Tristan and Isolde in Gottfried von Strassburg's 12th century version, a courtly romance in rhyming couplets. By this time, the 1850's, Wagner was also

---

[17] Entry: Tristan und Isolde.

influenced by the pessimistic, meditative moods of Schopenhauer's philosophy. But Tristan is about love...? You could say: the Tristan opera became a cross-roads of ideas: of having to abstain from love, of escaping from the world and living of love only, of the quiet life per se and of wishing to die. As I discuss below the loving couple's obsession with death is a bit sick. But *Tristan* can't be rejected for its unwholesome and indulgent sides; the music, as intimated, exquisitely mirrors the complex feelings.

Prose sketches of the opera were made by Wagner between 1854-1856. In August 1857, having got stuck about midway in The Ring, Wagner began to work in earnest on *Tristan and Isolde*. By September the libretto was completed. According to Wagner's memoir, *Mein Leben* (1870), he read it to an audience including his wife Minna, his "current muse" Mathilde and his future wife, Cosima von Bülow.

The composition of the music was done while Wagner had his love affair with Mathilde, from about October 1857 and to the autumn of 1858. If the affair was merely platonic or more hands-on we'll never know. Anyhow, Minna got air of the event, there were quarrels and domestic drama, and on August 17, 1858 Wagner had to leave both his wife and his mistress and move to Venice. There, during an eight-month stay, living in the Palazzo Giustinian, Wagner finished the score to the second act of Tristan. The third and last act was finished in Lucerne, Switzerland, August 1859. Wagner had returned to Switzerland because of fears of being extradited to Germany by the Venetian authorities, according to *Mein Leben*. Wagner at this time still was a wanted rebel because of his participation in the 1849 rebellion.

To stage *Tristan* proved difficult. As intimated in chapter 1 the Vienna Court Opera tried but failed to get it right, despite over 70 rehearsals between 1862-64. Finally, sponsored by Bavarian king Ludwig II, the première could be given on June 10, 1865, at the Munich Court Opera (*Hofoper*). But it wasn't easy then either, the music being complex and ahead of its time.

THE PLOT

Like *Lohengrin* and *Parsifal*, *Tristan and Isolde* elaborates on a tale to be found in conjunction with King Arthur and the Knights of the Round table. Tristan is somewhat peripheral to the Arthurian myth though.

Wagner's opera is about a loving couple, Tristan and Isolde, who can't have each other. Tristan gets the mission to propose to a bride on behalf of his lord, king Marke of Cornwall. When Act 1 begins we see Tristan and Isolde sailing back to Cornwall. But on the ship the bride, Isolde, falls in love with Tristan instead. Next the king marries Isolde but her secret affair with Tristan continues. In Act 2 the pair is caught in the act in the park of the royal castle. Tristan draws his sword and challenges the man who has led the king to the love nest. But in the ensuing duel Tristan lowers his sword and is severely wounded.

Act 3: Tristan goes off to live in his remote castle, waiting for Isolde to arrive and ease the pains. When she finally arrives Tristan is dead and then she, too, ends her life.

Needlessly Wagner in his scenario brought along the idea of a philtre making Tristan and Isolde fall in love. Originally this was a plot element to explain away to medieval audiences how a faithful vassal, Tristan, could do the unheard of act of falling in love with his lord's bride-to-be. We modern people don't need it to be told like this. We get it: the pair in the title aren't supposed to fall in love, it's a transgression of written and unwritten laws, but they do. But of course, the philtre is also a way of underlining the plot in a symbolic way.

So we have an impossible love story, a story of forbidden love, the enjoyment of a sweet pain that can only be fulfilled in death. This is what the overture is about, with its angst-ridden chord, the Tristan chord, and its ever-ongoing cadences that never seem to lead to harmony. This is also mirrored in the end's "Isolde's Love Death".

Tristan is an exercise in indulgence, taken to a higher level, about loving love for its own sake. And the Tristan music will live forever in its haunting beauty. *O höchste Lust, O Seeligkeit...!*

LOVE MEETING

Looking closer at the libretto I will focus on Act 2, where Tristan and Isolde is secretly in love while Isolde is married to king Marke. All of this act plays in the park before Isolde's chamber, in the night, with the secret love meeting of the pair as the centre of the action.

It all begins with Isolde asking her handmaid, Brangäne, if a certain hunting party of the king is safely off so that Tristan can come and visit her. When the coast is deemed clear Brangäne shall extinguish a certain torch which will be Tristan's cue. Impatient to meet her love Isolde sings:

> *O spare mir des Zögerns Not!*
> *Das Zeichen, Brangäne!*
> *O gib das Zeichen!*
> *Lösche des Lichtes*
> *letzten Schein!*[18]

Freely translated. "O spare me the pain of waiting! / The sign, Brangäne! / O give the sign! / Put out the last / gleam of the light!"

Finally Brangäne deems it right to extinguish the light of the torch. Tristan sees it and approaches the spot, an open place before Isolde's chamber adjoining the park. This scene reads like the balcony scene in *Romeo and Juliet*. They too meet in the night, fearing that daybreak would come, and on the way they exchange some memorable lines. And in Wagner's scene we have the pair singing in unison things like this:

> *Ist es kein Traum?*
> *O Wonne der Seele,*
> *o süsse, hehrste,*
> *kühnste, schönste,*
> *seligste Lust!*[19]

---

[18] Tristan und Isolde, p.18.
[19] Ibid p.20.

Freely translated: "Isn't it a dream? O sweetest pain, loveliest, wildest, highest, dearest lust!"

As I said, this is indulgence. You shouldn't promote indulgence, the enjoying of forbidden feelings per se, but along with the music with its "wavering tonality" this is quite an experience when seen on stage.

Tristan and Isolde love each other, loving love for its own sake, loving to live in dual ecstasy in the night. This is also rather sick: to haunt the hours of the night, performing deeds that stand not the light of day. They see themselves as married to the night:

O nun waren wir
Nacht-geweihte!
Der tückische Tag,
der neidbereite,
trennen konnt' uns sein Trug,
doch nicht mehr täuschen sein Lug![20]

Freely translated: "Now we are wedded to the night! The treacherous day, ready to hate, may divorce us but not deceive us."

This love of the night and the dark leads to feelings of death-wish and a nihilist craving for the tomb. There is no spirituality here, no "we'll meet again in heaven" or such. We only get, *Lass mich sterben! Nie erwachen!* Sick.

---

[20] Ibid p.23.

9. THE MASTER-SINGERS OF NUREMBERG (1868)

Among Wagner's operas meant to be performed in one night *The Master-Singers of Nuremberg* is his longest, being more than five hours long. Plot-wise it's a bit manufactured and elaborate, however still enjoyable for a modern audience. It's both pompous and light-hearted, both elegant and down-to-earth, being a realistic play set in medieval Germany. As for the music I like the overture, sporting a fugue inscribed into an orchestral score. This is solemn festival music, to me signalling "traditional holiday, pomp and circumstance".

MEDIEVAL NUREMBERG

In the 1840's Wagner took an interest in German literature, especially the 1500's and the figure of Hans Sachs (surname pronounced as "sax"). Sachs lived in the free imperial city of Nuremberg, a city-state with some independence under the crown of the Holy Roman Empire. Moreover, Sachs was a cobbler and a master-singer, occupied with the rules and customs of the singer's guild.

In reading about Sachs Wagner got ideas for a comic opera, the only one he wrote. The resulting work, *The Master-Singers of Nuremberg*, is down-to-earth and rather unheroic, having townspeople, artisans and workers in the leading roles, not larger-than-life characters as in Wagner's other operas. It's also interesting that Wagner, at the end of Act 2, has a brawl and a near-riot, the likes of which he had seen in Nuremberg in 1835 according to Mayer. You could say: Wagner was a romantic artist staging dramas about fairies, heroes and gods but he could also keep it real.

The actual work on *The Master-Singers* began many years after Wagner had read about Sachs. Only when *Tristan and Isolde* was done in 1861 Wagner took up *The Master-Singers*, first, as usual, writing a prose scenario. The libretto was begun in 1862 and the music was composed in the following years, during diverse problems (like bad prospects for The Ring, *Tristan* deemed impossible to perform, and separation from Minna who finally died in 1866). The première was given at the Munich Court Opera on June 21, 1868.

THE MODEL MASTER-SINGER

The plot is about a singing contest and a loving couple. The model master-singer Hans Sachs helps the budding singer Walther von Stoltzing to win both the contest and the bride.

As intimated, among his one-evening dramas *The Master-Singers* is Wagner's longest. Like all his operas it runs for three acts and the scenes are aplenty. However, it's a vivid play, as humorous as Wagner could be, the scenes breathing with the spirit of music. It's about singers, about the artisans' guilds of ancient Nuremberg being occupied with choir and solo singing. Wagner in his plot has captured two aspects of this culture, both the somewhat sclerotic adherence to rules as well as the anarchic spirit of composing freely.

So what happens? In Act 1 we learn that it's midsummer time in Nuremberg, a time of the year when the artisans' guilds stage a singing competition. The one who can deliver a song that's both original and adheres to the rules is crowned master-singer. The first scene shows us a church where there has been a service with the singing of a chorale. Now the church is to be the place for a test of hopeful singers, before the competition proper that's held the next day, midsummer's day.

A chance meeting is important for the plot: a young woman, Eva, having attended the service, happens to meet Walther von Stoltzing, a Franconian nobleman visiting Nuremberg. As is the rule in Wagner operas when "boy meets girl" they fall in love on the spot.

But how is Walther going to win her hand? By becoming a master-singer is the answer...! The one who wins the contest, Eva will marry; she has the option to refuse the winner but the bottom line is, a master-singer she wants. So when Eva and her maid has left the church Walther stays on to see the singers' trials. He is lectured on the art of master-singing and finally delivers his own song. For example he sings these lines about the charms of springtime in the woods:

So rief der Lenz in den Wald,
dass laut es ihn durchhallt;
und wie in fernren Wellen
der Hall von dannen flieht,
von weither naht ein Schwellen,
das mächtig näher zieht;
es schwillt und schallt,
es tönt der Wald
von holder Stimmen Gemenge;
nun laut und hell schon nah zur Stell'
wie wächst der Schwall! Wie Glockenhall
ertost des Jubels Gedränge![21]

Freely translated: "The spring calls in the woods, awakening it; in waves the sound floods every nook and cranny, the woodland swinging and dancing with lovely tunes, sounding gloriously like silver bells, rising in jubilation."

This is a song worthy its name, you might think. But the judge of the contest, the unimaginative Beckmesser, notes the many faults

---
[21] Die Meistersinger von Nürnberg, p.17.

Walther commits while singing, transgressions against the rules of performing of the singers' guild. So Walther's rejected, not being allowed to enter the competition. We also learn that Beckmesser too wants to marry Eva, whether he knows about Walther's interest for her or not.

What's the role of Hans Sachs in this? He is rather off-centre in the plot in Act 1, although he's there and exerts a certain presence. You could say that overall he has the role of MC, a Master of Ceremony and overseer of the plot, one that discreetly makes things happen.

EVENING

Act 2 plays in a city street, with the shop of Hans Sachs next to the house of Pogner's. Eva's father is the goldsmith Veit Pogner. It's evening and Eva, having learned of Walther's failure, now sits down with Sachs to discuss tomorrow's song contest. Sachs sits out in the open mending shoes; as mentioned above he's a cobbler by trade. As for the plot it seems like Beckmesser will win the contest but Eva doesn't want to marry him. She says: couldn't Sachs, being a widower and a skilled singer, enter the contest, so that she can marry him if he wins? But Sachs says that he's too old for her. Then Sachs describes Walther's failure at the trial. Eva gets upset and runs off, with Sachs drawing the conclusion that she truly loves Walther.

Just then Eva meets her maid, Magdalena, informing her of Beckmesser's plans to come and serenade her, that is, sing a love song by her window. Eva would rather not endure this; she goes off searching for Walther while Magdalena will pose as Eva at the bedroom window.

The action is rather tight in Wagner operas, you could say: eminently telescoped. Naturalistic traits like unfruitful searches, dead-ends and waits don't become the stage. This comes to mind when in the next scene Eva bumps into Walther; she doesn't have to search for him, he's just there. That's how it should be in an opera plot. Now, in view of Walther's rejection at the trial the two plan to run away, leaving town and go on living as lovers anywhere. But Sachs has overheard their plans. He has a better future in store for them and now he forces them to hide inside Pogner's house.

Next Beckmesser arrives, about to sing his serenade to Eva. But Sachs, still sitting by working, interrupts the song by his own singing and hammering on a pair of half-made shoes. Beckmesser tells him to stop but Sachs says that it's his, Beckmesser's shoes that he's about to finish, the shoes being overdue as Beckmesser had stated *en passant* in Act 1. It's agreed that Sachs will stop working on his shoes, but Sachs will instead act as a judge of Beckmesser's song by striking a sole with his hammer. Beckmesser is not amused but he doesn't have time to bicker as he now sees Eva in her window, not knowing that it's Magdalena in disguise.

Beckmesser starts singing his serenade. But he tends to make mistakes, formal errors of the kind a judge must mark in the realm of master-singing. In other words, Sachs gets a lot of opportunities to hammer on his soles—so much, in fact, that the shoes are completed in the process!

Next Magdalena's spouse David, Sachs' apprentice, sees Beckmesser serenading Magdalena. Jealous at this intrusion David attacks Beckmesser whereby the neighbours are awakened and other apprentices join in the fray. In all this Walther and Eva again try to run away, but now they are separated by Sachs who shoves Eva into her father's house and drags Walther into his own shop. Then, suddenly, the riot dies down and all is quiet in the nocturnal street.

ST JOHN'S DAY

It's morning the next day, being the *midsummer day* of heathen origin, in Christian lands such as Germany now—in 1550 and on—called St Hans Day, commemorating John the Evangelist. Otherwise midsummer of course is the time of the year when the day on the northern hemisphere is at its longest: the midsummer solstice. It's Hans' name day and the day for the singing competition, but the old man isn't happy. Sitting in his shop he muses over the riot and the vanity of everything—*Wahn! Wahn! Überall Wahn!* Thus begins Act 3 of the opera.

As you remember Sachs brought Walther along into his shop the night before. Now the master teaches the young man the spirit of master-singing. In order to win, Sachs says, Walther must somewhat approach the spirit of formal master-singing. Walther on the spot composes a new song and Sachs writes it down, however, the last verse is left undone.

The two men has left the room to dress for the festival. Beckmesser then enters the shop and sees the written-down song, guessing that Sachs is planning to enter the contest himself in order to win Eva's hand. Re-entering the shop and meeting Beckmesser Sachs denies that he's in for the contest, at the same time admitting that it's his hand-writing on the paper in question. Then he gives the song to Beckmesser, warning him that it's a tricky piece to sing. Beckmesser is nonetheless glad and sure of winning the contest now, having a song written by the master-singer Sachs himself.

In the next scene Eva arrives at the shop. Eventually Walther too enters the room wearing his finest. Glad at seeing Eva he completes the final verse of the song. Sachs blesses the couple and they're off for the singing contest. There Beckmesser fails miserably in singing the song he obtained from Sachs. How then, the audience asks itself, could a Hans Sachs song sound so miserable?

Walther is called forth to sing the song as it should sound. It's against the rules to have an eliminated contestant like Walther to sing at the contest, but the assembled townspeople allow it. And eventually they all love the song, being innovative while at the same time rooted in tradition. Walther is declared the winner and he gets the hand of Eva.

VIEWS

The very last lines of the opera have our MC, Hans Sachs, singing about the need for a German national culture. Wagner the young radical in time may have become more conservative but his stressing the need for a German way of singing and composing, in contrast to Italian and French styles, to me seems legit, even when Wagner said it in 1868. Both as a radical and a conservative Wagner held nationalist views and in this form, uttered by Hans Sachs, they seem to mirror Wagner's core sentiments. Remember that by this time there was no *Kaiserreich*, Prussia hadn't won its decisive victory over France yet, and nationalism still wasn't mainstream. By this time, 1868, nationalism was on the rise but it hadn't triumphed. So don't say that Wagner in this respect, in writing these lines sung by Hans Sachs, was an opportunist.

I mean, if Wagner hadn't said this, who would? Weber was since long dead by then and Liszt never talked about the need for a German national art. Neither did Brahms, Schumann or whomever as far as I know. Now, I freely admit that Wagner was no saint. For example he could be called a hypocrite in first revolting against the Prussian Wilhelm in 1849, the king helping the Saxon king to quell the 1849 rebellion, and then lauding the same person in his *Kaisermarsch* of 1871, when Wilhelm had become emperor. And Wagner's operas might mostly be in a sort of cosmopolitan, not folksy, style, but at the same time: he was right in saying "we are Germans, we have a peculiar style, we have the right to express it in music". Wagner was the most vocal advocate for these ideas in 1868. And in the words of Sachs this becomes:

> *Hab acht! Uns dräuen üble Streich'!*
> *Zerfällt erst deutsches Volk und Reich,*
> *in falscher welscher Majestät*
> *kein Fürst bald mehr sein Volk versteht;*
> *und welschen Dunst mit welschem Tand*
> *sie pflanzen uns in deutsches Land.*[22]

Freely translated: "Watch out! A strife is brewing. If the German people and country go down in a false, borrowed glory no prince will understand his people, with the German spirit dressed in an alien garment." Then this:

---

[22] Ibid, p.67.

Was deutsch und echt, wüsst' keiner mehr,
lebt's nicht in deutscher Meister Ehr'.
Drum sag ich euch:
ehrt Eure deutschen Meister,
dann bannt Ihr gute Geister!
Und gebt Ihr ihrem Wirken Gunst,
zerging' in Dunst
das Heil'ge Röm'sche Reich,
uns bliebe gleich
die heil'ge deutsche Kunst![23]

Freely translated: "No one any longer would know what is German and true, if it didn't live on in the spirit of the Master. Therefore I say unto you: honour your German masters, praise their good spirits! Even if the Holy Roman Empire crumbles the holy German art will remain, as long as it's praised by you!"

Thus we see the artist's perspective carrying the day: even though the Holy German Empire crumbles (as it had in 1805), as long as the German geist lives on we can be safe. This could be a memento for any time: politics and war aside it's art and the genius of the artist that is the true leader of the people. This Sachs intimates earlier in this aria: *Verachtet die Meister nicht, ehrt ihre Kunst!* More than the heroes of war and politics you should praise the artist who in his works of art embodies the people, the culture, the land and all. With this Wagner's seemingly opportunistic adherence to Prussia, Bismarck and the kaiser after 1871 becomes fully bearable. Like this: on the surface Wagner was courting to the political establishment but in the words of Hans Sachs he succeeded in putting the artist highest on the pedestal.

THOMAS MANN

German author Thomas Mann was an avid Wagner fan. Admitted, he was also critical of the composer. But in all he was enchanted by the Wagner oeuvre. And from his book on Wagner (*Wagner und unsere*

---
[23] Ibid.

Zeit, 1963, Swedish edition 1968) I quote the following, an eloquent praise of *The Master-Singers of Nuremberg*:

> ...*The Master-Singers* is a lovely work, truly a *Festspiel*, a poem where wisdom and audacity, the dignified and the revolutionary, tradition and future are unified in a radiantly happy manner, awakening one's enthusiasm for life and art. During personally sombre and heavy days it was born from the inner exultation of faith and power, and it will always awaken exultation...[24]

---

[24] Mann 1968, p.146; translated by the author.

10. THE RING OF THE NIBELUNG (1876)

With The Ring Wagner created a great work in several respects. First, it stretches over four full evening performances. True, the first part is "only" a foreplay but it still runs for 2 ½ hours. Secondly, The Ring has lived on ever since the first full performance in Bayreuth in 1876. This opera cycle nowadays is staged throughout the world, being the ultimate dream of every opera director. Every opera house with self esteem wants its own Ring. To oversimplify: why do you even build opera houses? Answer: to stage Wagner's Ring.

BACKGROUND

The opera *The Ring of the Nibelung* has four parts:

. *The Rhine Gold*
. *The Valkyrie*
. *Siegfried*
. *Twilight of the Gods*

As for composing it this can be said, the bare-bones facts of it being something of a repetition from chapter 1 of this book. In the early 1850's Wagner was living in exile in Switzerland. Here he began writing the prose outline and libretto for The Ring, completing it in 1852. The musical score for the first three parts, *The Rhine Gold*, *The Valkyrie* and more than half of *Siegfried*, was completed in 1853-57. Then the years went by with other projects. Finally, in 1871, Wagner got going with *Siegfried* again. In 1874 the music to the final part, *The Twilight of the Gods*, was completed.

The première of the complete Ring, with all four operas played in suite during four evenings, was given in Bayreuth in August 1876.

THE WORK

In The Ring Wagner brought together the Sigurd saga of The Poetic Edda with some threads from Snorre's Edda, plus the 13th century Volsunga Saga along with the southern German Nibelungenlied. These stories already were somewhat related, Wagner basing his work on an existing, interconnected mythic material, but his synthesis has in some ways given new dimensions to the whole. The portraits of the brooding ruler Wotan, the adventurer Brünhilde and the rebel Siegfried are viable re-interpretations of traditional archetypes.

There are some problems concerning Wagner's Ring, the way it stands. But I'll get to this later. Overall in this opera Wagner gives us a vision of how Wotan rules the world in relation to the Earth Goddess, the rest of the Aesir, humans, dwarves and Valkyries. Nietzsche for example was quite moved by the appearance on stage of Erda, the earth goddess. This had never before been seen on an opera stage, making it into a heathen mystery play of sorts.

So then, is The Ring pagan in structure and intention? Well, no. Wagner was no adherent to Asatru or something like that. He was no pagan. But in this work everything is archaic and old, Wagner at least not being a modernist destroyer like his latter-day interpreters and directors. However, they can do what they want, portraying it in modern clothes, glass and chrome; the core of the work is sound and can't be laughed off. In this *oeuvre* we get the whole spectrum of struggle, adventure, love, broodings over the world situation, insurgency and living in the wilds. The *forest* to me seems to play a major role, here in the form of the Germanic fairy wood, the timeless venue for all of our dreams and archetypes.

AN OVERVIEW

As a work of art The Ring is wide and deep, being both a symphonic piece and a literary epic. Also, it has philosophical depth. So an overview of its myth, ontology and characters is sorely needed.

In his book *Trollkarlen från Bayreuth* (*The Wizard of Bayreuth*, 1989) Ingvar Lundewall makes an overview of all of Wagner's *oeuvre*. As for *The Ring of the Nibelung* Lundewall goes into some length in summarizing this opera's mythical foundation, world of ideas and personal gallery as well as the music with its consistent use of leitmotifs. At the end Lundewall stresses the musical, artistic qualities of it. Apart from all the ideological superstructure The Ring is, after all, a work of art and not a scholarly lesson:

> Ideas, theories and analyses whether *Der Ring des Nibelungen* is a problem play or a political or aesthetic revolution drama, a logically rigorous antique tragedy or a mosaic pattern, a romantic fairytale drama, an opera or a "music drama" – all alternative interpretations lose every sense in the dark of the opera salon, as soon as Wagner the Shaman exerts his magic on stage and in the orchestra pit.[25]

This must be remembered, not only when looking into The Ring but into all of Wagner's works. As I just said, "consistent use of leitmotifs." According to Lundewall this applies to approximately the first half of this musical quadrology. But in the second half Wagner is forced to patch things up with his musical phrases. It all becomes an end in itself, beyond dramatic function and context. The critic Eduard

---

[25] p.134; my English translation.

Hanslick pointed this out back in the day. Sometimes Wagner even put together quite divergent leitmotifs, like "the love motif of the Völsungs" with "the motif of the horse Grane", this being quite bizarre and pointless as Lundwall suggests.

INTERPRETATIONS

Now for Lundewall's survey of The Ring. The focus is on the deeper mythical meaning of it but other traits are also discussed.

Diverse interpretations have been made of this play, Lundewall says. For example by George Bernhard Shaw (1856-1950), the Irish playwright. In his mind Siegfried is Bakunin the anarchist while Wotan stands for church and state. Loge, an intermediary, stands for the academic sharing his knowledge. Alberich is the capitalist, running a mining company. I'd say: this isn't totally off the mark. The revolutionary Wagner of 1848 vintage somehow thought along these lines and even met Bakunin in Dresden these days. This political interpretation isn't *the* answer to it all but you have to admit, The Ring indeed has some radical political DNA in it. Interpretations: we also have a dyed-in-the-wool communist one, an East German staging that Lundewall mentions, one where Siegfried and Hagen are seen as heads of rivalling Nazi organizations. This may be seen as a thing of the past, of the simplistically politic 1970's. But maybe left-leaning producers and directors tend to see Wagner's work as downright fascist even today. You never know. I even admit it myself sometimes, saying for example that the Third Reich had Wagnerian traits, as I discuss in chapter 15. But artistically speaking, to stage The Ring with black uniforms and chauvinist pomp is not the way to go, I think. It would be an overstatement, not efficient scenographically.

According to Lundewall The Ring essentially is about the attempts of Wotan, Alberich and the giants to change the conditions under which the world, the whole of existence, is functioning. For different reasons they want to liberate themselves from the basic, material law of necessity, from the Erda regime dictating the rule of elements and the succession of seasons. Wotan seems to put up a resistance against predestination; he's against having men's lives judged by the Norns and the end of the world being pre-ordained.

CIRCLES OF EXISTENCE

There are four circles of existence in The Ring, Lundewall says: the natural, the mythical, the human and the heroic.

> The *natural* has the four elements represented by Erda and her Norn daughters (earth), the Rhine Maidens Woglinde, Wellgunde and Flosshilde (water), the fire-spirit Loge (fire) and the woods dwelling bird (air).

According to Lundewall this is Wagner's Erda: she has created the world, pre-ordained what's going to happen and even fixed the destruction of it all. She forces everything to obey the rule of necessity. Like the Norns she can predict the future but is unable to change anything. Erda is mirrored in the vala (seeress) of The Older Edda, prophesying the end of the world (in part three of the opera even Erda herself is addressed as "vala"). Erda normally is inactive, immanently influencing all things alive, but is awakened when called. This happens twice in The Ring. When Wotan in Act 3 of Siegfried awakens Erda he wants to gain knowledge, like Odin in *Sången om Vägtam*.

The Norns in Wagner's epic have no names but are called Urd, Verdandi and Skuld in the Edda. They have a marginal role in The Ring but represents predestination, cutting the life thread for each person. The other elementary spirits also know the future but can't interfere: the Rhine Maidens and the bird of the woods all proclaim the truth, either being believed (the bird) or ignored (the maidens). As for animals Lundewall notes other symbolic appearances of them in Wagner's operas, like the deer in *The Fairies*, the swan in *Lohengrin* and *Parsifal* (and *Wieland the Smith*), and Siegfried recalling his dead mother when he sees a hind in a wood. The look in the animal's eyes brings him back.

Loge as a fire spirit may not have so much in common with the ancient Nordic Loge, at least not on the surface. At the same time the Loge we meet in the Edda is false, rich in ideas and elusive and the same goes for Wagner's version of Loge. Wagner in my opinion has successfully adapted this intriguing character for the stage.

WOTAN

Now on to the second circle of existence in The Ring, called the *mythical*. It's made out of the Asa gods, primarily their father Wotan, accompanied by his wife Fricka.

A defining character of the Nordic *Odin*, *Wotan* in German, was to be a war leader. And this is intimated in The Ring where he calls the völsungs and the Valkyries to battle. Other than that he's a wanderer posing questions to those he meet, obliquely letting them know that he is the father of the gods. This is also mirrored in The Ring, like when Wotan meets Mime in *Siegfried*. Mime can't answer Wotan's question who's going to reforge the sword Notung (since it's Siegfried). And in The Poetic Edda a similar mystery-laden dialogue is in *Vafthrudnismál*: at the end this dwarf, Vafthrudnir, from Odin gets the question of what he, Odin, whispered in the ear of Balder before he was laid on the funeral pyre.

This according to the venerable Lundewall. Then he crucially notes: the overall impression of Wotan throughout The Ring is a whiner regretting his faulty decisions, a brooding intellectual henpecked by Fricka. This is true, and Wagner's Wotan can be criticized for more, but for the time being I think: Wotan in quarrelling with his wife might, for better or worse, also become relatable to a modern opera-goer. And that said, in truth Lundewall also stresses the truly godlike impression of Wotan in *The Valkyrie*, when he takes leave of his favourite daughter having put her inside the ring of flames.

Wotan seems to be powerless, confronting the law of necessity drawn up by Erda and executed by the elements of nature and the passage of seasons. To be a truly cosmic god Wotan must replace the rule of necessity with that of free will. This paradox is rather elaborate, to me reminiscent of a mystical Christian world-view: God has abstained from some of his power so that his children, mankind, can choose him and freely wander towards the light instead of the dark. And this, choosing the light, they will probably and eventually do since their souls are made of the same light as God. But if man wants to choose dark then it's part of the school of existence.

True, there is nothing of this in The Ring. But Wotan planning to install Free Will as a new, impelling force of the cosmos, either isn't a part of Asatru, not being anything we find in the Eddas. Correct me if I'm wrong.

Part of Wotan's plan of becoming a more powerful god is to have intercourse with Erda in order to engender the Valkyries, and then making a deal with the giants to build him the Valhalla castle. There the Valkyries will gather the fallen heroes that Wotan needs for the final battle of world domination, the fateful battle of Ragnarök.

Wotan has also engendered Siegmund to be raised as an independent man, bearer of the idea of free will, the new guiding force in existence. This is said to be a way to stop the preordained downfall of the gods, unclear in what way. Anyway, it all comes to a head when Siegfried, Siegmund's son, with his sword breaks Wotan's ruler spear: free will has conquered and the Erda law of necessity is nullified, Lundewall says. And this was what Wotan wanted. However, at the same time Wotan realizes that free will brings with it murder and treason, something he hadn't counted on.

Lawlessness is out and about. And Wotan himself never stopped grieving about having transgressed the law when getting hold of the Rhine Gold by theft. Thus he is again convinced of his failures and thus he no longer fears the downfall, in fact he welcomes it. *Amor fati* takes hold of the master indulger.

ALBERICH

Like Wotan *Alberich* is an ambitious fellow, wishing to become more than what he is. Alberich's way is to renounce love in order to let his power-lust reign freely, cursing love in order to gain worldly power. And when he loses the Ring he curses it, the curse thus affecting Mime and Hagen. The latter is Alberich's son.

Then Lundewall mentions two other circles of existence, the human and the heroic. I treat them both as one here, overall rather summarily.

Siegfried is something of an *Übermensch*: he knows how to reforge the sword Notung, knows how to defeat the dragon, and he goes unscathed through the ring of fire and kisses Brünhilde. Siegfried is the agent that will realize the plan of Wotan becoming the ruler of the cosmos with the help of free will, hindering the downfall of the gods. But lies and machinations, treason and fraud are also about now and spells the end of Siegfried.

There seems to be nothing left of the free will. For example, Gunther and Gutrune in *Twilight of the Gods*, at first have no malice afterthought in what they do. But they are drawn into the intrigues and thus are reached by the curse of the Ring, eventually committing crimes so that they must be punished. And at the end, when the Ring is returned to the Rhine Maidens by Brünhilde, this isn't enough: she casts fire towards Valhalla, igniting it. The curse of the Ring is nullified by the cleansing power of the flames. Gods and men, dwarfs and giants, fish and fowl, plants and trees—everything perishes in a cataclysm. Kind of an overstatement. The fiery end, the cosmic downfall is all in the Edda, but Wagner's idea of having free will in a prominent role could make you hope for more than this archaic, fate-bound end.

IN THE EYE OF THE RING

That was Lundewall's survey. But more could be said in sketching the background for The Ring. For instance, there's an undated one hour video in circulation dealing with Wagner's Ring. *In the Eye of the Ring* is the title and in the beginning is given another ontological survey of this Wagnerian work, plus some more mythical background. I find this video most enlightening, filling in some gaps that Lundewall's survey may have left out.

This Ring video starts by saying that in western philosophy there are four elements, earth, air, water and fire. In Wagner's epic earth is represented by Erda, the earth goddess, water by the Rhine nymphs and fire by Loge, the god of fire. Okay, I just mentioned this above. But this video is original in saying that Wotan represents air.

Wotan is a somewhat airy character in this context, being a brooding, thinking man, "inclined to intellectual speculation", this in contrast to his more practical, down-to-earth wife Fricka, having a predilection for convention and lacking feeling and intuition. From the well beneath Yggdrasil Wotan drinks wisdom, gaining insight, having to relinquish his one eye to pay for the drink. Wotan, according to the video, represents *thought*. On the other hand Erda, the Earth goddess, represents *intuition*. Erda has three daughters in the form of the Norns, the three fate goddesses. The first recalls the past, the second sees the present and the third, the future. The Rhine maidens, the water spirits, are said to represent *evolution* and *nature*. Like the sirens of ancient, Greek mythology the Rhine maidens are teasing and alluring beings, leading men astray with their song, as they do with Alberich at the epic's beginning.

Next this video tells us:

> Fire is ambivalent. It is at the same time destructive and life-giving, consuming and purifying.

The symbol for this is, as stated earlier, Loge, the video in question saying that he's "...a character as engaging and elusive as flame itself."

To be flaming is to be quick and smart, putting an end to deliberations and systematic thought, and Loge is all that.

The world as a whole is represented by Yggdrasil, the world tree, "an intermediary in contact with the four elements." At the foot of the tree the Norns spin the tread of destiny. The lives of men are ordained by fate and ruled by the sequence of seasons, as men were during the stone age.

This world is populated by the Aesir of which Wotan is the father. Below, on earth proper, there lives the two giants Fafner and Fasolt, said to represent two aspects of mankind: Fasolt is simple, good-natured and poetic, symbolizing a sort of every-man, while Fafner is "suspicious, destructive and selfish" and thus a symbol of everything bad in a person.

NIBELUNGS

In the depths of the earth we have the Nibelungs, industrious workers symbolizing wealth, greed, industrialism and technology. Foremost among them is Alberich, motivated by "potent sexual energy", being drawn to the Rhine nymphs but instead deciding to steal their gold. Renouncing love he ventures on a quest for world domination by forging a magical helmet and ring.

Freia is also mentioned, the goddess of love. She plays a minor part yet love proper plays an important role in the epic, such as when Siegfried and Brünhilde (and Siegmund and Sieglinde) fall in love. Violence is symbolized by Donner, the god of thunder and war. Donner is called *Tor* in Norse mythology; a certain *Tyr* was the war god proper but Tor also was something of a war god.

BALANCE

According to *In The Eye of the Ring* Wagner's epic is about the balance of the world being disturbed. The balance is the elements, the succession of seasons and Yggdrasil watching over it all, having at its root the well of wisdom. The tree is rooted in earth, has its branches in the air and is watered by rain.

According to the video and based on Wagner's libretto, the first transgression of this world order by Wotan was this: to drink from the well of wisdom. The second was when Wotan broke off a branch of Yggdrasil. Wotan makes it into a spear, carving it with powerful runes, the symbol of his ambition to rule over men and gods. These two transgressions (drinking from the well, breaking a branch off the tree) has these consequences:

> The contaminated water of the well ceases to sing as the well dries up. The tree perishes from its wound. Time stops flowing. Soon the thread of destiny will break. It is the beginning of universal pollution.

Then we have the role of Freia's gold apples, playing some part in *The Rhine Gold*. The apples grant the gods eternal youth. Freia herself, however, is given as a pledge before the payment is given to the giants for building Valhalla. This gives Fafner control of the apples, thus depriving the gods of their immortality. However, "Loge will find a way to redeem the pledge": he knows about the Rhine Gold treasure.

This is the background to events when the opera begins. The video in question summarizes the pre-plot situation succinctly: "The giants set to work. Wotan dreams of his fortress. Fricka has nightmares. Dawn is near."

WOTAN'S QUALMS

I'll soon relate all of the plot of The Ring, but *In the Eye of the Ring* also has this to say about Wotan's psycho-social situation throughout the drama.

Wotan eventually steals the gold from Alberich in order to pay the Valhalla building giants with it. He then has qualms about having stolen the gold, in the words of *In the Eye of the Ring*:

Wotan finds himself with no way out. Either he can return the ring to the Rhine Maidens by stealing it from Fafner, and lose his power by breaking the treaty (violating his own laws of society by committing theft), or he holds off and falls under the curse, because he has profited from the theft which has payed for the castle. What is worse, if Alberich, who does not suffer the same legal and moral constraint, found a ruse to take the ring, that would be the end of the god's power. The power of the ring might overcome the might of the spear.

Within the narrative logic of The Ring this could be good to remember.

KEY SCENE

In the Eye of the Ring also has this to say, about a key scene in Siegfried.
   Siegfried, Act 3: Wotan is first elated of the news that Siegfried has killed the dragon, taking the Rhine Gold treasure, and that the hero is off to meet Brünhilde. "The couple of the future will be his heirs and will save the world."
   Siegfried on his way to Brünhilde then meets Wotan, who is out to congratulate his son. True to his enigmatic style Wotan poses Siegfried questions, an approach that Siegfried dislikes. The young man is ebullient after having killed the dragon and enters a quarrel with this old man. In the ensuing battle Siegfried breaks Wotan's spear with his sword. Wotan flees. This is all a symbol of a new emergent spirit, a free and intuitive humanity asserting itself against the old order of convention and sterility.

- - -

After all this background, are you ready for a summary of the plot? I think you are. The mythology, psychology etc. of The Ring is a tough subject and I'm not done yet; I'll return to it at the end of this chapter, delivering my final judgement on the subject. But until then, let's look at what The Ring tells us story-wise, from beginning to end.

THE RHINE GOLD

The Rhine Gold is a foreplay to the Ring epic. *The Rhine Gold* is a one act-drama consisting of four scenes: in the river Rhine, on a plain before Valhalla, in a subterranean cave-dwelling and finally on the plain before Valhalla again.

The Rhine Gold tells how the gold of the Rhine Maidens is stolen and brought into the world of men and gods, the treasure bringing death and destruction in its path. He who covets the gold comes under its spell: in order to own it you must relinquish love.

The opera begins under the surface of the Rhine. Three water nymphs, the Rhine Maidens, swim about playing with each other. The first lines sung in the opera are these, by Woglinde:

Weia! Waga!
Woge, du Welle!
Walle zur Wiege!
Wagalaweia!
Wallala weiala weia![26]

Further on I will translate the quotes but this is almost untranslatable, well-sounding nonsense poetry mimicking the movement of waters and waves (Ger. *Welle*).

The maidens are suddenly accompanied in the water by the dwarf Alberich. They tease the newcomer and he gets aroused, wishing to have these fair damsels for his company. But then he sees the Rhine Gold on a rock above the waters. The women tell him of the nature of the gold: he who takes it and makes it into a ring will gain earthly power, but in the process he must renounce love.

---

[26] Das Rheingold, p.1.

Nothing else? Alberich says, swims to the surface and steals the gold. Laughing he disappears beneath the ground to his smithy. The Rhine Maidens looks despondently on, lamenting and singing their "Wallala, Wallaleialala…"

- - -

In his smithy Alberich makes himself a helmet and a ring of the gold. He reigns in Nifelhem exerting control over its dwarves, the mining, treasure-hoarding Nibelungs. Hence the title of the entire opera: *Der Ring des Nibelungen*; Nifelhem is a mist world and in German mist is *Nebel*. And *ungen* means "offspring, children of" etc..; hence the title can be interpreted as "The Ring of the Fog People", if you need to have it spelled out literally.

With his magic helmet and ring Alberich now is invincible: he can become invisible and transform himself into whatever he wishes, such as a dragon. But we're not there yet. In the plot proper, right after Alberich has stolen the gold, the scenery shifts to scene two, a mountain plain before the Valhalla castle.

OUTSIDE VALHALLA

Outside Valhalla the gods, led by Wotan with his wife Fricka, awakens. Half-asleep Wotan thinks about this castle where he will reign:

Der Wonne seligen Saal
bewachen mir Tür und Tor:
Mannes Ehre,
ewige Macht,
ragen zu endlosem Ruhm![27]

Freely translated: "The beautiful, graceful hall / guarded by wall and gate: / manly honour, / eternal power / shining in endless glory!"

---

[27] Ibid p.12.

This abode, Valhalla, is built for the gods by the two giants Fafner and Fasolt. As pay for their job they have gotten Freia, the goddess of love. She now prays to Wotan: let me go, let me be free of this plight! Also, because Freia is captured she can no longer give the gods their golden apples keeping them young. The gods already feel their strength leaving them. Another payment has to be considered.

The god Loge has a clue. He's a devious god of flames, a jester and a trickster, a heathen Lucifer. His name (Icelandic *Loki*, Swedish *Loke*, German *Loge*) indeed derives from *flame*, German *Lohe*, Swedish *låga*. Having been around in the world Loge for example knows that Alberich has stolen the Rhine Gold. Even though the owner of the gold must renounce love, this Alberich fellow seems prepared to do that. Loge sings:

Nur einen sah ich,
der sagte der Liebe ab:
um rotes Gold
entriet er des Weibes Gunst.
Des Rheines klare Kinder
klagten mir ihre Not:
der Nibelung,
Nacht-Alberich,
buhlte vergebens
um der Badenden Gunst;

das Rheingold da
raubte sich rächend der Dieb...[28]

Freely translated: "I only found one who despised love; for red gold he discarded womanly charms. The daughters of the Rhine deeply lament: in vain Alberich asked for the embrace of the bathing. Enraged he then stole the Rhine Gold."

Loge intimates that the gold should be given back to the maidens. But when hearing that Alberich has indeed made a ring of

---
[28] Ibid p.20-21.

the gold, Wotan wants it: *Den Ring muss ich haben!* ("I must have the ring!") And with Loge's advice to use cunning Wotan is convinced that the gold treasures of Alberich should be stolen, to use as payment for the building of Valhalla. At the same time Wotan can steal Alberich's ring of power and keep it for himself. Wotan and Loge bid farewell of the gods and leaves for Nifelhem.

NIFELHEM

The action in Nifelhem is the third scene of the drama. In this cave world, with its treasures, mines and smithies, the two gods first meet Mime, a slave dwarf who has forged the wondrous helmet of the Rhine Gold. This helmet, allowing the bearer to transform into whatever shape he wants, is now carried by Alberich, the capitalist parody that rules Nifelhem by plaguing his vassals to dig for gold and hoard it in the cave rooms. He exerts power with his ring. Another result of the theft from the Rhine Maidens: of the gold Alberich has forged a ring, one that makes everyone bow before its wearer.

And now the two Aesir, Wotan and Loge, have visited this cave dwelling. Next Alberich comes fort; in seeing the pair he's suspicious of them but Loge intimates that he is his friend. Not only is he the god of flames, he *is* the flame that, among others, the smith Alberich uses when he's forging his heirlooms. He is the flame that lights his way and warms him. Loge:

> *Kennst du mich gut,*
> *kindischer Alp?*
> *Nun sag wer bin ich,*
> *dass du so bellst?*
> *Im kalten Loch,*
> *da kauernd du lagst,*
> *wer gab dir Licht*
> *und wärmende Lohe,*

wenn Loge nie dir gelacht?
Was hülf dir dein Schmieden,
heizt ich die Schmiede dir nicht?
Dir bin ich Vetter,
und war dir Freund:
nicht fein drum dünkt mich dein Dank![29]

Freely translated: "Don't you know me, you quarrelsome dwarf? Indeed, who am I? Who gave you warmth and illuming flame in your dark abode, if not the smile of Loge? Who helped you to forge, who heated the furnace? I'm your friend and helper but you're most ungrateful."

Loge doesn't really want to befriend Alberich, this is just a ruse to prepare the ground for the stealing of the gold. Loge, ever so courteous, then asks the dwarf of his magic helmet. What can he do with it?

Alberich says that he can transform himself into a dragon. This he does.

The wily Loge says he is impressed. But can't Alberich also transform himself into something really small...? This the dwarf also can, turning himself into a frog. Then Wotan captures the frog. Having regained human form Alberich is forced, held by Wotan, to give away his helmet and his ring. Relinquishing the objects the dwarf shouts a curse after the gods, saying that the Rhine Gold from now on will only bring misery to its owner.

But Wotan and Loge don't listen on that ear. They head back to the plain before Valhalla, the same as in scene two. Now they can pay the giants with the gold. But the builders must have it all, even the helmet and the ring: the prerequisite was that they were given as much gold that would cover Freia. And to be completely covered Wotan must give away the helmet and the ring too.

---

[29] Ibid p.33.

ERDA'S ADVICE

Wotan giving away the ring is a fine scene in this opera. The giants say that they want the ring. The other gods—Donner, Fricka, Froh and all—tell Wotan to give away the ring. But if he gives away the ring he loses its promise of worldly power. The argument is brought home by the earth goddess, Erda, who now rises from the ground and is visible from the waist up, as we read in Wagner's stage directions. They also say that she is of noble stature, sporting flowing dark hair. Pleadingly stretching out her hand to Wotan she sings these memorable lines (my free translations in brackets):

Weiche, Wotan! Weiche!
Flieh des Ringes Fluch!
(Fall back, Wotan, fall back!
Flee from the curse of the ring!)

- - -

Wie alles war, weiss ich;
wie alles wird,
wie alles sein wird,
seh' ich auch:
(I know how everything was,
is and will become:)
der ew'gen Welt
Ur-Wala,
Erda mahnt deinen Mut.
(Erda, the eternal seeress
of the world beckons you
to gather your wits.)

- - -

Doch höchste Gefahr
führt mich heut
selbst zu dir her!
(Greatest danger now brings
me to you.)
Höre! Höre! Höre!
Alles was ist, endet!
Ein düstrer Tag
dämmert den Göttern:
dir rat' ich: meide den Ring.
(Hear me: all things must pass.
A sorrowful day brings the
twilight of the gods:
My advice to you is,
give away the ring).[30]

Then Erda disappears and Wotan changes his mind, deciding to follow her advice. The giants already have the assorted gold treasure and the helmet and now, at long last, Wotan throws the ring on the heap. Freia is released and the gods regain their strength. And immediately the giants start to quarrel about the gold treasure. It ends with Fafner killing his brother.

The curse of the gold is at work. Wotan wisely nods: *Furchtbar nun / erfind' ich des Fluches Kraft!* "Fearsome is / the curse of the ring!"

Fafner gathers his treasure in a sack and tramps away. But Wotan isn't relieved by this: he knows that he and Loge in the first place stole the gold from Alberich: *Mit bösem Zoll / zahlt' ich den Bau!* ("With a wicked due / I payed for the hall!") But eventually he's placated by Fricka, showing him how welcoming the castle sits in the evening glow. Moved Wotan sings:

Abendlich strahlt
der Sonne Auge;

---

[30] German text, ibid p.47-48.

in prächtiger Glut
prangt glänzend die Burg.[31]

Freely translated: "The eye of the sun / shines in the evening. / In mighty glow / the radiant castle stands before me."

Truly, such a splendid keep must be a safeguard against the forces of darkness! And with his wife and all the gods Wotan finally traverses the rainbow bridge to the castle. Only Loge stays a little behind, prophesying the downfall of the gods. And in the background, from the Rhine that floats out of sight, the lament of the Rhine Maidens is heard, wishing to have their gold back. When the gold was in the river it was pure; now, being brought into the world, it brings nothing but misery. Doom and gloom, that's how this otherwise promising foreplay ends.

THE VALKYRIE

The second part of The Ring is called *The Valkyrie*. It's an opera in three acts, each with about three scenes. Act 1 plays in the dwelling of Hunding, in a memorable house built around an oak. Act 2 plays in the wilderness and Act 3 on the top of a mountain. It's a drama about Wotan's deliberations, about the mother and father of the hero of the next operas (Siegfried), of the god-sent sword that Siegfried also comes to use and of Brünhilde, the Valkyrie, the daughter of Wotan who also plays a part in the following two operas.

Wotan hasn't sat idly since last we met him. For instance, with the earth goddess Erda he has engendered a memorable company to guard Valhalla, *Valkyries*, supernatural women who are tasked to retrieve fallen human fighters to Valhalla, the heathen heaven of Nordic lore. Wotan also needed someone to defeat Fafner and reclaim the treasure, so with a mortal woman Wotan has begotten the promising son Siegmund. Ignorant of his god-like origin he will grow up as the stepson of a gamekeeper and his daughter, Sieglinde.

---

[31] Ibid p.51.

In his youth Siegmund has to witness how his sister, Sieglinde, is abducted by the hunter Hunding. He swears that when he comes of age he will liberate his sister. One day he gets some help from the gods. It is Wotan who has submitted him a note saying that he will send him a mighty sword to help him the day he needs it. When Siegmund grows up he sets out on his quest. This is the proper beginning of *The Valkyrie*: with Siegmund entering the strange woods dwelling, the house built around an oak. There he meets a blonde woman and a strong hunter. It is Sieglinde and Hunding. Not recognizing them he tells them about his search.

By this Hunding understands who Siegmund is, in essence, a member of a hostile family. Curiously, however (to a modern mind), Hunding lets the man stay for such is the Germanic hospitality. But at dawn, they fight! Hunding says:

Mein Haus hütet,
Wölfing, dich heut;
für die Nacht nahm ich dich auf;
mit starker Waffe
doch Wehre dich morgen...[32]

Freely translated: "My house, young cub, / will protect you now; / for the night I'm your host. / But tomorrow arm yourself / with good weapons..."

Siegmund goes to bed by the fireplace in the house. He recalls the promise by Wotan, writing the note saying that he will give him a sword one day: *Ein Schwert verhiess mir der Vater, / ich fänd es in höchster Not.* "My father promised me a sword, / being in dire straits I would find it." And truly: at night Siegmund, sleeping by the hearth, gets a visit from Sieglinde who says there is a sword to be found in the house. When she was wedded to Hunding in this very house a stranger entered, an old man with a wide-brimmed hat covering one of his eyes, the other shining fiercely. In other words, it was Wotan.

---

[32] Die Valküre, p.8.

Next during that fateful visit Wotan took out a sword, thrusting it into the bulk of the tree, burying it to the hilt: *(Das Schwert) stiess er nun / in der Esche Stamm, / bis zum Heft haftet es drin*. Now Sieglinde shows Siegmund the sword in the oak: like Excalibur in the anvil it's fixed and seemingly impossible to be removed. Only the right person can pull out the sword, the woman says. But Siegmund is the right person: he takes the hilt, starts to pull and easily manages to release the weapon. It is Wotan's sword Notung, this he understands, the weapon that his father had promised to send him.

BRIDE AND SISTER

Siegmund and Sieglinde then fall in love. They also understand that they are related; Sieglinde is *Braut und Schwester*, bride and sister. The opera doesn't elaborate on the taboo of incest. Instead, the relationship in question to me symbolizes *forbidden love*, a known Wagner theme: we also saw it in the play *Das Liebesverbot* (*The Ban on Love*), an unsuccessful Wagner opera from 1836, and in *Tristan and Isolde*. To love and being forbidden to love because of social or blood-related barriers, creates mental strains that Wagner found it inspiring to compose music about. This interest in forbidden feelings might also be labelled as "indulgence". But if it engenders music like that in *Tristan*, I say: Okay.

The pair decides to flee, thus it will be less bloody and more in accordance with the laws of hospitality; because, on the other hand, to kill a man that has given you shelter—as Hunding indeed had— would be sacrilege. Moreover, there is the opinion that Sieglinde now can be considered to belong to Hunding; this the goddess Fricka says, having ventured out from Valhalla to judge in this delicate affair. She now prevents Wotan to send a Valkyrie to help the young couple. This Valkyrie, Brünhilde, thus continues with her ordinary day job, to retrieve fallen warriors to Valhalla. On the way, however, some way into Act 2, she spots Siegmund and Sieglinde in a mountainous region where they have fled. They are now detected by Hunding who's going to kill them. Brünhilde sympathizes with the couple. She decides to help Siegmund in the duel against the hunter when Wotan appears; he puts his spear over the hero's blade enabling the hunter to kill Siegmund.

This was done to maintain justice as outlined by Fricka: Sieglinde was considered to belong to the hunter after all the years she had lived with him. But Wotan is remorseful and his anger now is transmitted to Hunding, who falls dead to the ground after having been reached by the god's lethal gaze. Brünhilde knows that she's in trouble, she has violated Wotan's orders by helping and feeling sympathy for Siegmund and Sieglinde. Retrieving the hero's corpse she lifts it up on her horse and flees. On a lonely place she buries Siegmund. But Wotan is following her, being angry at this disobedience. Brünhilde is accompanied by some of her Valkyrie sisters. To them she sings these melodramatic words:

Der wilde Jäger,
der wütend mich jagt,
er naht, er naht von Norden!
Schützt mich, Schwestern!
Wahret dies Weib![33]

Freely translated: "Wrathfully the Lord of the Hunt chases me, from the North he approaches. Guard me, sisters, save this woman!"

PUNISHMENT

When Wotan is near the Valkyries run off. We are left with Wotan and his favourite daughter whom he now has to disown. This is the final scene of the opera (Scene 3, Act 3); Brünhilde had promised not to meddle in the Hunding-Sieglinde-Siegmund triangle but she did anyhow and now she has to suffer the punishment.

---
[33] Ibid p.47.

Wotan, heart-stricken yet fatherly and godly, dooms her to sleep an enchanted sleep. Anyone who can wake her up can have her for bride. By this she will have lost her semi-divine status, becoming merely human. Brünhilde understands as much. But being of a proud warrior nature she asks this of her father: she wants to be awoken by the bravest man there is. Wotan sees to it that her enchanted sleep is executed within a circle of tall flames. Only the bravest warrior can venture into this ring. With the help of Loge, the Asa god with a close relationship to fire, fire is stricken out of the rock. A ring of flames rises up surrounding Brünhilde, who is already asleep.

The final lines of The Valkyrie, with the flames being conjured up and all, sound like this. Wotan, having placed Brünhilde on a rock and covered her with her shield, says:

Loge, hör!
Lausche hieher!
Wie zuerst ich dich fand,
als feurige Glut,
wie dann einst du mir schwandest,
als schweifende Lohe;
wie ich dich band,
bann ich dich heut!
Herauf, wabernde Lohe,
umlodre mir feurig den Fels![34]

Freely translated. "Loge, hear, waver forth! Like once I found you, as a fiery glow, evanescent in your incandescence; like I bound you then I bind you now! Come here, wavering flame, encircle in blazes the rock!"

And so the flames arise, encircling the rock and growing into a sea of fire. Making a sign with his spear Wotan says that those who fear the spear of Wotan won't break the ring of fire. But to this the orchestra plays the Siegfried leitmotif, intimating that the hero of the

---

[34] Ibid p.63.

next opera indeed will rise to the occasion, enter the fiery sea and liberate Brünhilde. Before that Siegfried has also, literally, broken the spear of Wotan. This Wotan secretly wished, for already in *The Valkyrie* (Act 2, Scene 2), he longs for a hero who "in his wildest obstinacy is faithful to the god". This sounds like a paradox and isn't fully worked out conceptually, however it hints at some philosophical depths that Wagner was capable of. The scene in *Siegfried* with Wotan meeting Siegfried after the hero has killed the dragon is one completely out of Wagner's imagination, a scene of powerful mythic quality in itself, showing how man liberates himself from the sclerotic rule of a possibly senile ruler.

However, this all comes to naught as the world perishes in the last opera in the cycle, making it all end on a sombre note. Necessity and nature—pure matter—triumph over freedom and heroism. Still, as I said, Wagner had some depth and the ethic-ontologic meaning of being a hero of the Siegfried kind is portrayed vividly.

SIEGFRIED

Opera number three in this suite is called *Siegfried*, sporting three acts with three scenes each. Act 1 is in Mime's woods dwelling, Act 2 plays in the desert realm of the dragon Fafner and Act 3 is about what happens the hero, Siegfried, next, having killed the dragon.

Act 1 brings us to Mime's forge, deep in the woods, the anvil and the rest being placed in a cave. By this an old acquaintance is again brought into the action: Mime, the former vassal of Alberich who found the Rhine Gold and brought it into the world of dwarves, gods and men. Mime played a supporting role in *The Rhine Gold*, as you might remember.

As a dwarf skilled in forging Mime now has built a forge in the forest depths where he begins to forge a sword with which Fafner is to be killed—Fafner, the giant who took hold of the Rhine Gold and still protects it in a desolate land, himself turned into a fierce dragon. Mime wants the treasure for himself. Mime's plan is to recruit a hero to fight for him with a promise to get the sword but in the end, after the deed, Mime will kill the hero and take the gold. Where then will he get his fighter? By coincidence, one day a feeble woman with an infant in her arms had arrived at the forge. It was Sieglinde, Brünhilde having helped her to escape sometime in the latter part of *The Valkyrie*. Sieglinde became pregnant after she and Siegmund had been together while on the run. In the forest hut Sieglinde then told Mime that her child was called Siegfried, being of heroes' kin, the grandson of Wotan. She suggested that when she had died this hero would make Mime great services. She also gave him the shards of Notung, the sword wielded by Siegmund that was broken when Wotan put his staff across it.

The woman died and the child grew up with the dwarf. Thus the opera begins, with Mime trying to reforge Notung: only this weapon will do: *Ein Schwert nur taugt zu der Tat, / nur Notung nützt meinem Neid*. But the dwarf can't make it work. Who will again weld the parts together? Mime gets the selfsame question from Wotan, who happens to visit him in scene two. With usual mystique, rather well translated onto the opera stage, Wotan is out wandering and now he drops by at Mime's cave. The dwarf doesn't want his company but Wotan (only calling himself "Walker", *Wanderer*) starts a conversation, letting the dwarf ask him whatever he wants. Mime then asks Wotan about gods, men and giants, mirroring a similar gnomic dialogue in The Poetic Edda, *Vafthrudnismál*. In Wagner's hands this is a fine scene, archaic and yet with full bearing on the plot proper. Overall Wagner's treatment of Asa gods on stage may have been only partly successful but he had his fine moments too in this respect, the Wotan-Mime dialogue being one of them.

Next Wotan gets to ask the dwarf his questions, like what the sword is called that will bring down Fafner. Mime says: Notung. But who will reforge it? This Mime doesn't know.

FAFNER

The Walker takes his leave. Finally it's revealed that Siegfried will weld the broken sword into a fully functional weapon. Having finished the forging the hero tests Notung against the anvil and the anvil splits. Next, the dwarf and the hero are off into the wasteland to kill Fafner.

This, in other words, inaugurates Act 2 of the opera: the killing of Fafner. This was a dense, dramatic-poetic highlight of the original Volsunga Saga and the opera scene in question fully does it justice. Having arrived at Fafner's cave (there are many caves in this story) a heroic duel human-dragon takes place. And in the end Siegfried buries the sword in the dragon's body. The dragon however warns him of the curse of The Rhine Gold before he dies.

Siegfried also gets this tip from the dragon: to roast and eat his heart. Having done this Siegfried suddenly understands the speech of birds. This comes in handy when Mime presents him with a chalice of poisoned wine; just as Siegfried is about to drink it a bird in a tree warns him of the brew: "Mime wants to kill you and take all the treasure for himself," the bird says. Siegfried then has had enough of his foster father, killing him. The bird now says he's got a reward for the hero who has liberated the world from an evil creature. And over the lands the bird flies, followed by Siegfried: *Wohin du flatterst, / folg' ich dir nach!* ("Where ever you fly / I'll follow!")

INVOKING ERDA

Now we get to Act 3. It begins with Wotan, out for a walk in the woods. By a cliff he invokes Erda, the earth goddess. We saw her in *The Rhine Gold* and now it's time for her second (and final) appearance in the cycle. The words of Wotan invoking her has some power:

Wache, Wala!
Wala! Erwach!

Aus langem Schlaf
weck' ich dich schlummernde auf.
Ich rufe dich auf:
Herauf! Herauf!
Aus neblicher Gruft,
aus nächtigem Grunde herauf![35]

Freely translated: "Wake, vala, vala wake up! From a long sleep you are soberingly awakened. I call you: get up, get up! From misty depths, from the nocturnal lands, get up!"

But when Erda finally awakens nothing really comes of this conversation. In age-old managerial style she refers the errand to another level, her daughters the Norns. These goddesses of fate will know what will happen. But the Norns are ruled by necessity, Wotan says; he wants her, Erda's wisdom.

Erda again refers to another department, this time Brünhilde. But what may Wotan's own daughter teach her father?

This whole scene is something of a grandiose failure, symbolizing that Wagner didn't really know what to do with the gods, especially Erda, when he had put them on stage.

Personally I'd say: Mother Earth is still around and she knows a lot, being wisdom incarnate. Admittedly, Wagner intimates that she knows more than the secrets of the bare elements, of Earth proper which is her name; Erda = Earth. But nothing of this is showcased in this scene. The Ring universe is rather primitive: necessity rules in the form of nature's laws, seasons follow seasons and nothing can be done against that. Wotan, wishing to impose some higher order on this is seen as a transgressor, like when he broke a branch off the world tree Yggdrasil to make it into his ruler's spear. Because, the making of the spear damaged Yggdrasil so that it began to wither, this we will know in the final opera of the cycle, *Twilight of the Gods*. A rather despondent world-view. But maybe that's the inner logic of the Aesir universe.

---

[35] Siegfried, p.42.

FATEFUL MEETING

Another fateful meeting follows. When Erda has again disappeared under the ground, giving Wotan no clue as to the development of the world, Siegfried approaches the wilderness where Wotan stays.

As intimated this meeting has its original approach. Wotan meets the victorious Siegfried, his grandson, but the youngster grows suspicious of the old man and his inquisitive style. When Wotan bars the way with his spear Siegfried breaks it with Notung. There's some symbolical power in this: the free spirit of man breaks out of the mould of necessity. To challenge a god in this way seems a bit nihilistic but the scene yet makes some sense, within the logic of Wagner's drama. A pity though that Wagner makes nothing of it: Wotan has more or less wished this development, he had in *The Valkyrie* wanted a man to rebel against him, and now Wotan simply picks up the shards of his spear and heads back to Valhalla—and there he will build a funeral pyre of the wood of the chopped down Yggrdrasil...!

Wotan himself never returns to the drama after this. In *Twilight of the Gods* he is only mentioned in third person. And the opera cycle ends with a glow in the background, symbolizing the flames consuming Valhalla.

The Ring ends in a slightly messy fashion. Any elevated idea of freedom, of ruling the world in accordance with morally consistent laws, based on an esoteric ontology (God is light and men's souls are fragments of that light), of breaking out of the bonds of nature, of being anything more than a slave under the passage of the seasons—any such idea is quelled. Erda rules, the Norns decide the length of men's lives, any one with any ambition of raising himself out of this quagmire fails; truly, a primitive world view. But as intimated, the Aesir universe might demand a fiery end, this being spelled out in the Edda itself.

- - -

To repeat the plot, in this scene two of Act 3: along the road Siegfried meets Wotan who wants to question him. Siegfried doesn't recognize his grandfather and virtually says, "Get away, old man!" Wotan then crosses his path with his spear: *[S]o sperre mein Speer dir den Weg!* But Siegfried chops it apart with his sword. Wotan sees himself defeated, a god by a man. Siegfried has challenged fate—and won…? In any case he next comes to Brünhilde, sleeping inside the ring of flames. Fearlessly he enters the flames, kisses Brünhilde and awakens her. They take a liking to each other. Brünhilde, already an outcast from the world of the gods, now wants to live as a human with Siegfried.

TWILIGHT OF THE GODS

Now for the last opera in the cycle: *Twilight of the Gods*, sporting three acts with many scenes. Mostly it's a tedious plot, devoid of godly presence. I mean, I truly enjoy the earlier parts of the cycle. There was some promise in the air then, it was gods and men in a sensible plot. Now we get the messy, fourth and final part of the opera. Even musically this is evident. In the earlier parts the leitmotifs made sense, even when two leitmotifs were coupled together, but in the last drama Wagner couples anything just in order to make it work in some or other fashion. But, as Lundewall intimates, what does the pairing of "the love motif of the Völsungs" and "horse Grane" mean? Nothing.

Twilight of the Gods begins in grand, mythic style with the goddesses of fate, the Norns, sitting on a mountain spinning the threads of life for men. There is something of "the witches of Macbeth" in this, archaic and alluring, but only slightly. I mean, the Norns are seen as the rulers of men's lives and what's the meaning of that for modern man? We are free men, we have free will. Now Wagner comes and tells us that everything is pre-ordained. The Norns cutting a man's life thread is a final decision, no appeal can be made. That may have been the world view of heathen northern Europe but to a modern man this is nonsense. With his will he can raise himself out of necessity and act according to the moral examples of Buddha, Christ and Socrates.

HAPPENINGS

The Norns get to tell us the latest plot developments. As intimated Wotan has grown tired of everything; for example, he could never get over the fact that he stole the gold from Alberich. Wotan has let raw power be the foundation of his grand castle, Valhalla. Then an earlier deed, his making of a spear of one of Yggdrasil's branches, has hurt the tree and now Wotan has ordered it to be cut down:

Da hiess Wotan
Walhalls Helden
der Weltesche
welkes Geäst
mit dem Stamm in Stücke zu fällen.[36]

Freely translated: "Then Wotan ordered the heroes of Valhalla to cut down the withered world-oak, branches, trunk and all."

The wood from the tree will be a funeral pyre for the gods along with Valhalla. Nothing matters anymore: his spear was broken by Notung and then the rule of Wotan was at an end anyhow. Even though he *wanted* Siegfried to rebel in this way...?

It's all a mess, I'm sad to say. The Ring is still a classic performed all over the world but it doesn't cohere.

The Norns, crying despondently over the fall of everything, is part of a foreplay of this opera. Also part of the foreplay is the next scene, with Siegfried and Brünhilde having spent the night in a cave. Siegfried gives Brünhilde the golden ring of the Nibelung treasure as a token of their love. He then takes his arms and his horse, Grane; on a raft on the Rhine he heads off to new adventures, in truth to misery and doom. This takes place to the tune of "Siegfried's Rhine Journey", a bright and heroic piece. Wagner in his private notes says that after this he left the composing of the work for a while, not knowing how it would proceed musically. But after some 15 years Wagner gathered himself and set music to the end of it, a story rather much in the vein

---

[36] Götterdämmerung, p.2.

of the Nibelungenlied. Now it was all court intrigue and doom, mostly okay in the view of what has gone before—I mean, you have to tie up the threads in some or other way—but as intimated The Ring is an unfulfilled promise and *The Twilight of the Gods* is my least favourite part of the cycle.

THE GIBICHUNGS

King Gunther rules the tribe of *Gibichungs* on the River Rhine. His half-brother Hagen Gronje, the son of the evil Alberich, hears about Siegfried and learns of his condition. Hagen wants the gold treasure and gets an idea, advising Gunther to find a wife for himself and a husband for their sister Gudrun. Brünhilde thus could be Günther's wife and Siegfried Gudrun's husband. Gudrun is given a philtre she can give Siegfried so that he forgets about Brünhilde. Under the influence of the same drug Siegfried will arrange for Brünhilde to be given to Günther. Gudrun and Günther both agree to this plan.

Siegfried arrives at the kingdom of the Gibichungs. He is received by king Gunther and also meets Gudrun, who gives him the love potion. He now forgets Brünhilde completely. So when Gunther talks about this woman Siegfried promises to win her for Gunther, who is now his blood brother.

As you recall, a magic helmet was forged by Alberich and then taken by Siegfried from Fafner when the dragon was dead. This helmet in German is called *Tarnhelm*, usually translated as "magic helmet". It can transform the wearer, as when Alberich transformed himself into a dragon before the Nifelhem-visiting Wotan and Loge; Tarnhelm is also an invisibility helmet. *Tarnung* is German for "protection, camouflage"; a camouflage smock, for example, is a *Tarnkappe,* and a ship made invisible from radar with stealth technology, in German is a *Tarnkappenschiff*. Anyhow: Siegfried now owns this helmet. And to help his blood brother Günter he now puts on the magic helmet and assumes Günther's figure, arriving at Brünhilde's cave and taking her gold ring. He brings her to the real Gunther to become his wife and then assumes his true form as Siegfried. When Brünhilde now sees the ring on Siegfried's hand she understands the betrayal: she has been tricked by her former beloved. Carelessly Siegfried goes off to the court, accompanied by Gudrun.

Once in the castle king Gunther holds a party to celebrate the upcoming wedding with Brünhilde. She now hates Siegfried and becomes easy prey for Hagen who plans to get his hands on the ring. He fools Brünhilde into believing that Siegfried wilfully has deceived her (when in truth he was affected by the philtre). A small incident could be arranged at the next day's hunting excursion. Brünhilde is totally in on this plot.

THE HUNT

Act 3; the end of the whole Ring cycle is near...! When the hunt begins the next day Siegfried is separated from the others. The chasing after a bear leads him away into a forest and on to the banks of the Rhine, back to where it all began in part one of the cycle, with Alberich stealing the gold from the Rhine Maidens. Now Siegfried meets the three water spirits, sitting on a rock in the river.

Right before Siegfried enters the stage the Rhine Maidens get to bask in the sun, again singing their enchanting *Weialala leia, wallala leialala...!* And this:

Frau Sonne
sendet lichte Strahlen;
Nacht liegt in der Tiefe:
einst war sie hell,
da heil und hehr
des Vaters Gold noch in ihr glänzte.
Rheingold!
Klares Gold!
Wie hell du einstens strahltest,
hehrer Stern der Tiefe![37]

---
[37] Götterdämmerung, p.35.

Freely translated: "Mother Sun sends her beams; night rules the depths: once they were light, when wholesome and holy the gold of the Father still shone in them. Rhine Gold, bright gold! How bright you once shone, holy star of the depths!"

Then they hear the hunting horn leitmotif, a Siegfried leitmotif. Ever since first appearing in the beginning of *Siegfried* he has carried a hunting horn which he blows heroically now and then. And when the hero himself now comes sauntering along the Rhine beach the three water nymphs say hello and strike up a conversation. Seeing the ring on his finger they recognize the Rhine Gold shimmer in it, saying: give it back! But Siegfried refuses, stating that he has won it in lethal combat against the dragon Fafner.

They talk and bicker, the dialogue being rather resilient in true Wagner fashion, weaving the fates of gods, elementals and men into a relatable narrative. The only thing that lets it down is the doom and gloom atmosphere; I know, that's the way of the Nordic epics, but as intimated I don't see the point in telling a story with a world view of "nothing works, nature takes its revenge". It's like cultural Marxism elevated into a Nordic myth.

Siegfried again refuses to give the maidens the ring. Then they say that the ring is cursed and will lead him to destruction. The hero laughs it off and moves on. But the hero has been secretly followed by Hagen Gronje. In a crucial moment he throws a spear that fells Siegfried. Hagen is just about to take the ring off the dead when he sees king Gunther and his retinue arriving. Caught in the act...!

Brünhilde for her part now realizes the Hagen plot: it's the curse of the ring that's the root of it all. King Gunther promises to punish Hagen. Siegfried is put on a shield and carried down to the beach. There, he is placed on a bonfire. Since Brünhilde has lit the funeral pyre she unites herself with her lover in the flames: *Selig grüsst dich dein Weib!* ("Blessed your woman greets you!")

Everything ends where it began, with the Rhine, the three water nymphs riding a wave that carries with it Siegfried's and Brünhilde's bodies, the gold ring being repossessed by the trio. Hagen can't resist the sight of the glimmering treasure and tries to get his hands on the ring: *Zurück vom Ring!* This is the last line sung in the opera. But Hagen is pulled down into the depths by the maidens. Thus the ring also sinks into the Rhine, the treasure being reclaimed by the river nymphs, its rightful owners, and since then the Nibelung ring has never been seen in the lands of men.

FLAMES

I'm getting ahead of myself; there are some additional events that need to be related in The Ring finale.

While Siegfried's pyre burns we have seen how Valhalla is ignited in the background. Actually Brünhilde has given the cue: when lighting Siegfried's pyre she shouts to Wotan's two messenger ravens, which happen to be nearby, to fly to the cliff where she once lay among the flames; the flames still burn there, thus Loge, the god of flames is still there, and thus the ravens will alarm him and show him the way to Valhalla: *[W]eiset Loge nach Walhall!*

In this way Loge reaches Valhall which is lit. As indicated earlier Wotan wants it, having stacked up his own funeral pyre in this castle of his. In this way he takes the consequences of his failed mission as a ruler. Thus Wagner connects the rightful reclamation of the Rhine Gold with the end of gods and men, having this symbolizing the end of the world as described in the Edda, the *Götterdämmerung* of the "Prophecy of the Vala". If this plot move is justified, I don't know, it gets a little too theatrical and telescopically contracted, this connecting of the end of the world to the Rhine Gold story. And in The Poetic Edda the real Wotan, that is, Odin, dies not by lying down on a funeral pyre but by fighting with the wolf Fenrir, who devours him.

Wagner's end to his epic is a great conflagration. And maybe he thought it justified since he tied the beginning of the epic, the discovery of the Rhine Gold, to the advent of the world of gods and the building of Valhalla. The story seems to require such a grand finale whether the mythical foundation admits it or not. The Edda, one of Wagner's sources, undeniably has its Armageddon but I figure it will come later, at the end of time.

Then again, to have this opera end in fire and destruction might seem logical, given the pessimistic tenor of the work. Necessity rules, The Norns decide the lifespans of men, and no one—no god, no man—may rise above that iron law in order to do anything, be it "raise mankind from the level of animals" or "as a hero mould your life according to your will".

THE MUSIC

As we've seen The Ring is a drama, full of learning and intrigue. But let's not forget the musical side of it.

In The Ring we have orchestral pieces like "Siegfried's Funeral March", pompous and gripping in spite of its fragmented structure of leitmotifs stacked on top of each other. We also have "Siegfried's Rhine Journey", truly heroic and bright, and "Waldweben", an alluring symphonic poem impressionistically painting the image of a Nordic wood, the German wood as a timeless archetype.

The lyrical episodes of The Ring, the musical episodes free from song, philosophy and psychology, is what brings the listener along, what charms him: pieces like "Waldweben", the Rhine Music, the anvil music of the Nifelhem dwarfs and the etheric Valhalla theme.

The most famous orchestral piece from The Ring is "The Ride of the Valkyries" from *The Valkyrie*. I admit that I grew a little tired of this one some years ago. It became a little worn out. Now I can only say, in delving into the Wagner works before writing this book I've once again come to like it. It's warlike and pompous, it's about going into battle. And battle and violence aside it truly lifts you up. It's got the Wagner tuba at the forefront, a special, high-pitched tuba that Wagner invented.

The Ring is a musical treasure house. You could say: music holds The Ring together, not psychology, mythology and ontology.

GODS ON STAGE

As for an overall summing up of The Ring I'd say: don't write stories about gods. It's hard to make it work.

This is my advice to budding authors of the mythical kind, writers wishing to stage dramas with gods in them. I mean, let the dreams live, let fantasy and impossible visions dance around in your epics, but as for having gods as characters in a story it's not to be recommended. The gods may figure as an invisible presence, they may even make special appearances here and there, but to have them in the centre of a story and letting us partake of their everyday problems and broodings, this takes away their uniqueness.

You might see where I'm heading. Wagner, in writing an epic about men, elementals, giants and gods, was over-ambitious. I mean, it's okay having heathen Northern heroes doing their thing but then to also have Odin along takes the project into another realm entirely. In the old sagas like Volsunga Saga Odin definitely is around, however, only briefly, in chance encounters as The Walker. We don't follow him around. The human drama takes centre stage: the drama of Siegfried. Wagner started out writing a Siegfried opera (*Siegfried's Tod*, 1848) but then he got ambitious and wanted to put everything in there: The Poetic Edda, Valhalla, gods and the whole heathen cosmos.

It's okay to be inspired by old Nordic legends. And Wagner had his moments with the Aesir, there being some sublime moments in The Ring, moments that are credible even from the divine point of view (like Wotan and Loge visiting Nifelhem, the gods deliberating before entering Valhalla, Wotan taking farewell of Brünhilde). But overall the god part of The Ring is a mess, Wotan not being wholly credible as a god we get to meet and follow around.

As a comparison I'd say that Tolkien made it all work. Tolkien also read the Edda, Nordic sagas etc. but he took it to another level. At the same time he restrained himself, not having gods in the lead roles. The divine creatures (like Tom Bombadill) only figure briefly. The ubiquitous Gandalf also might be some sort of divinity (a "Maia" in Tolkien lingo) but this isn't said out loud in the narrative proper.

Moreover, the Lord of the Rings battle between Light and Dark is something 21st century man still can relate to (like Sauron seen as globalist materialism and the fellowship of the ring as an alliance between spiritualists, nationalists and friends of freedom) while Wagner's obsession with the elements, men's lives being governed by nature and fate goddesses is redundant. In Tolkien the individuals make a moral choice, that between good and evil – and good wins, in a cosmic end game. In Wagner the will of the individual is blown away in the torrent of the elements; nothing works, nothing matters, evil in the form of greed and the power of the gold conquers.

ODIN

Of course you have to try anything. I know about artistic freedom. But The Ring doesn't cohere, the philosophy being a patch-work of promising ideas that doesn't fuse into a story that means anything.

You could say: Wagner was good at absorbing things. The ideas of the 1848 revolution, Schopenhauer's philosophy, Arthurian legends, any old legend; these ideas he could fuse into operas that still work on their premises. Now, The Ring also fuses a lot of ideas and sometimes successfully so, but altogether it's something of a mess. Wagner worked with The Ring from the late 1840's to the early 1870's so he had time to leave it completely, not even deciding to finish it. But he kept going. He didn't see the faulty, irrelevant philosophical foundations of it. As intimated an epic about Aesir from the building of Valhalla and to "the end" does seem to require doom and downfall, but why even go there? In his next opera Wagner absorbed Christianity and made a more constructive story, all things considered.

Wagner was a good storyteller but he should have thought twice before he decided to tell us his version of how Wotan fails as a superior god. The Wagner version of Wotan is half-baked. The Odin of Nordic myth was (to follow the lead of Jesse L. Byock) the god of *war, wisdom, ecstasy and poetry*. But he was not the god of law, as Wagner makes him into. Okay, Odin guarded the moral of men but more in a, say, common law fashion. And as for his spear Gungner this, in the Nordic sources, seems to be more of an attribute of a war leader than the sign of a law-giver and cosmic ruler, as Wagner intimates. Gungner was known for never missing its target; clearly a war weapon.

On the other hand, Wagner's Wotan more seems like Zeus, the chief god of the ancient Greek pantheon. And—I'd say—philosophically the Greek pantheon might be easier to relate to for modern man than the world of Aesir, no offense. The same pattern that Wagner was embroiled in (the elements, the urge to raise above them, having mankind to break free of necessity) is there, in Greek mythology, in the form of Uranos as the primeval god, the god of the invisible presence, of heaven, space and *akâsha*. Then he begets the son Kronos, the god of elemental earth (not to be confused with Chronos, time); then Kronos begets Zeus, the god of law and ordered society, and he in turn begets Prometheus who gives fire to man and lets him rise above the power of the elements. Zeus then punishes Prometheus for this but in the end they are reconciled. Man by then is slightly freed from the power of necessity, not having to live eternally as a stone age cave-dweller, instead with the knowledge of fire as the symbol of being able to master his environment. In time the road is open for man evolve into a tool-maker, a city-builder, an artist and a philosopher. Truly a more inspiring synopsis than having everything fall because of "the power of gold, the power of the elements".

As for the Prometheus story Aischylos made it into a cycle of dramas of which part one survives, *Prometheus Bound*. Here we saw a drama with gods, on stage, relatable for the random theatre goer. And you have to admit: Wagner sometimes reached the heights of Aischylos' pathos. And in that Wagner is unique among *any* artist of our age. In the genre of "stories about gods", written today, no one comes even close. I hereby note this while at the same time I can't endorse The Ring as *the* masterpiece of our age.

TOLKIEN

I mentioned Tolkien above. To repeat: overall Tolkien made his work cohere, it still makes sense today—light versus dark, remember—whereas Wagner's work is something of a curiosity in linking stone age submission under the elements with modern ethics, lacking the acute metaphysical framework to make it all interplay and say us something.

Another aspect of the difference between Tolkien's and Wagner's artistic approaches is this.

Tolkien took a look at ancient myths, constructed his own more or less original mythology based on it and eventually made it all into a plot that modern man can relate to. Wagner tried to do the same. Wagner however stayed within the framework of The Edda, the Aesir and all. Tolkien went a bit further, making his own mythology. This act of Tolkien, this creating of an own fairy-world with mythical species, lands, languages and even its own creation myth, might seem a ludicrous, or harmless, pastime for a professor of philology. But it's more than that. The mythological world Tolkien so dearly but privately made up eventually came to artistic fruition, there for all to see. For when he was triggered by Allen Unwin to tell a story about his wondrous world, the Middle Earth framework became *a structure he could be free in*. And in large part because of this he made his ensuing work of art, *The Lord of the Rings,* cohere. That's the heart of creativity, of the process of making art: to create a structure within which you can be free. Tolkien in this respect succeeded but in The Ring Wagner didn't. That's why The Ring is something of a failure.

11. PARSIFAL (1882)

Parsifal was Wagner's last opera. I have issues with it, see below, but on the whole it's rather remarkable. There's nothing like it in the history of opera. The music is discreet, the plot is simple on the surface but rather elaborate, and the three acts balance each other perfectly. It's an opera with a thorough spiritual atmosphere.

MEDIEVAL EPIC POEM

The opera *Parsifal* is based on the medieval epic poem *Parzival* by Wolfram von Eschenbach. According to Wikipedia[38] Wagner read this poem in 1845. The themes of compassion and self-renouncing that may be found in Parzival then led Wagner on to Schopenhauer's ideas of asceticism and renouncing the world, which this philosopher had gotten from Buddhism. Wagner actually started to sketch an opera based on the life of Buddha, *Die Sieger (The Victors)* in 1856. But, as Mann says in *Wagner und unsere Zeit,* Buddha proved to be a little too perfect to stage a drama around.

However, an opera with a pious theme seems to have settled in Wagner's mind. A trigger in the process was this, with Wagner in 1857 seeing the springtime greenery outside his Swiss cottage, the one on the Wesendonck estate. In his memoir he said it was on Good

---

[38] Entry: Parsifal/Wagner opera.

Friday but Wikipedia (with Cosima Wagner's diaries as source) adds the info that this is conjecture, it was just a spring day that made the composer think how Good Friday should be. Anyhow, Wagner was out taking a stroll, seeing the garden "radiant with green", the birds singing and all being peace and quiet. And linking this to the role of Good Friday in *Parzival* Wagner started to occupy himself with that poem again, which he hadn't done since he read it in 1845. A prose sketch was made, outlining the drama in three acts.

The following years Wagner completed *Tristan* and *The Master-Singers*. Only in 1865 did he take up *Parsifal* in earnest. Now he made a detailed prose draft, outlining the plot, the characters and themes of the drama. Then The Ring had to be finished. Finally, after the first full performance of The Ring in 1876, Wagner turned his mind solely to *Parsifal*. By April 1877 the libretto was finished. Then the music was composed, being completed by January 1882. The première was given in Bayreuth, July 26 the same year.

SYMBOLISM

Parsifal is on the outset a clear-cut, three-act drama. The music is simple but not simplistic; Nietzsche was wrong in calling it "county-fair music". The staging is condensed and reduced; however, this drama also reeks of mysticism and esotericism.

At the same time the elaborations on the metaphysical—or rather, material—meaning of the Lord's supper are a bit primitive. It's Wagner's bent for symbolism that rules here, for better or worse. Generally Wagner's operas are fine displays of symbolism but in this case, *Parsifal*, I can only say that this mysticism about drinking wine-as-blood goes too far. Maybe I'm not a Christian at all since my opinion is that you can raise yourself spiritually by force of will, not by drinking blood. At the same time "Jesus Christ" is a complex phenomenon that, among other things, is symbolized in the chalice, the wine, the blood and all and *Parsifal* presents this to us. The symbols have an esoteric meaning.

I'm not wholly taken in by *Parsifal* but the main question is this: is there another stage-play around with such modern yet enjoyable music, with such pious atmosphere, with such mythical individuals in a relatable plot? No, there isn't. *Parsifal* has its flaws but it's still a timeless classic. Also, among Wagner operas it's rather unique in ending on a positive note. The play ends displaying a living, breathing ensemble mentally raised by the Christ impulse in the wonders of Good Friday. The actors don't, as otherwise is the case in Wagner operas, fall down dead. Okay, Kundry dies. But the overall spirit of the end is one of triumph and spiritual fulfilment, not doom and despair.

From a purely dramatic point of view this play is very concise. It has three acts: the first and last playing at the Grail Castle, the second at the castle of the evil Klingsor. Parsifal in Act 1 meets the Grail Knights but he doesn't understand what they are doing. In Act 2 Parsifal goes to Klingsor's castle and retrieves the spear. And in Act 3, after several years have passed, Parsifal returns and can cure the sick king of the Grail Knights with this spear.

As intimated I don't buy this magic idea of being saved by drinking the blood of Christ, which is programmatic and stated throughout the play. But overall *Parsifal* catches a mystic feeling like few other dramas, whether plays, operas, novels or epic poems. Of course Wagner was using a medieval story, a renowned classic (*Parzifal* by Wolfram von Eschenbach, 13th century), but he sure knew how to stage narratives in a relatable way, accompanied by hauntingly simple music.

THE GRAIL

As I said above *Parsifal* has three acts, at the Grail castle in the beginning and the end and in the middle at Klingsor's castle. This is a charming symmetry. Moreover, the different scenes in each act merges effortlessly into each other.

In Act 1 we get the Grail castle situation presented: here the Grail knights live, guarding the spear that the legionnaire Longinus thrust into the side of the crucified Jesus, and the chalice in which Josef of Arimatea is said to have gathered up the blood gushing forth after this thrust. However, the Grail knights have lost the spear to Klingsor, a knight having been discarded as unworthy of the Grail order. And in duelling with Klingsor at his castle the Grail king, Amfortas, has received a wound that won't heal. Amfortas was preoccupied with seducing Klingsor's woman Kundry, having put away the spear; this made it possible for him to be hit by his own spear.

To this plagued Grail castle now comes a foolish young man. His entry is memorable: the Grail knights have seen a swan being shot down. And the shooter is a mindless youngster armed with a bow, boasting that he can hit anything while in flight: *Im Fluge treff' ich, was fliegt*. The spokesman for the knights, Gurnemanz, admonishes him:

Unerhörtes Werk!
Du konntest morden, hier im heil'gen Walde,
des stiller Friede dich umfing?
Des Haines Tiere nahten dir nicht zahm?
Grüssten dich freundlich und fromm?
Aus den Zweigen, was sangen die Vöglein dir?
Was tat dir der treue Schwan?
Sein weibchen zu suchen flog der auf,
mit ihm zu kreisen über dem See,
den so er herrlich weihte zum Bad.
Dem stauntest du nicht? Dich lockt es nur
zu wild kindischem Bogengeschoss?[39]

Freely translated: "Crime unheard of! You've committed murder in the quiet temple of this wood. Hasn't the animals of the wood approached you tamely, greeting you piously? And from the trees you were met by birdsong. What had the swan done to you? In flight he was seeking his wife in order to circle with her over the lake, inviting them to a bath. This didn't move you: you only lusted for a foolish play with the bow."

---
[39] Parsifal, p.7.

This is a Christian story but one with elements you don't find in the Bible: the presence of nature in the form of a wood and kindness to animals. That's what this quote symbolizes to me.

When hearing Gurnemanz and seeing the dead swan before him, Parsifal breaks his bow and throws away his arrows. But when interrogated he's still mindless, unable to answer where he's from, what his father's name is and what he himself is called; the latter we only learn in Act 2. But he knows that his mother's name was Herzeleide ("heartbreak") and that he himself made the bow in order to protect them from the wild eagles of the wood. Eventually we get to know that Parsifal's mother wanted to safeguard her son from becoming a knight like his father, who died on a mission. Nonetheless Parsifal left his mother and went out in the world, fighting against wild animals and sturdy champions.

Essentially Parsifal is pure and honest but still he's like a nature's child, not exactly knowing good from evil. Like when the Grail knights take the Eucharist he doesn't understand anything of it. Then Gurnemanz chases him away, contemptuously advising him to keep away from swans and instead keeping company with geese.

Another important person in Act 1 is Kundry. In the beginning this woman has approached the Grail castle bringing balsam for the wounded Amfortas. Not that it helps; not even Kundry is bent on helping—*Ich—hilfe nie* ("I—never help") as she says. Soon we get to know that she's also a seductress and a witch. Still her presence is tolerated, this enigmatic woman that is a mix between Mary Magdalene, one of Jesus' followers, the Venus of *Tannhäuser*, Heroidas (the woman in the Bible saying "bring me the head of John the Baptist") and Ahashverus, the wandering Jew. Kundry namely has laughed at the crucified Christ and for this she has been punished with being unable to cry and lament, she can only scream and laugh. Her fate seems to be to wander along until doomsday, not finding solace anywhere.

For the plot it's also interesting that she has known Parsifal's mother, having been present at her death. Herzeleide died longing for her son and this is now held against him.

THE QUEST

Act 1 ended dubiously, leaving everything undecided: who is Kundry? Will the Grail king ever be cured of his pains? What will Parsifal do next?

Things get a little clearer in Act 2 although everything still is implicitly enigmatic, saturated in mythical feeling. Now we are at Klingsor's castle. This Klingsor fellow is somewhat like Alberich in The Ring, having renounced love in order to gain worldly power.

Klingsor converses with Kundry; here the mysterious woman is the servant of the bad guy. We learn that she will entrap the most dangerous champion of them all, Parsifal, because he is something of a fool, *ihn schirmt des Torheit Schild:* "he is protected by the shield of foolishness". He's innocent and at the same time a bit mad, impossible to figure out for a rationalist like Klingsor. Although a fool Parsifal, by the purity of his nature, seems to be chosen by the Grail to be its champion, and now he will approach Klingsor's castle and regain the spear. But maybe Kundry can steer him away from this; that's Klingsor's plan.

Next they see him approaching, Parsifal. He fights off the defenders of the castle. Then he enters a rose garden where another of Klingsor's traps await, in the form of *the flower girls* who try to ensnare him with their charms. They all say, "let me love you" and Parsifal plays along. But in the end he grows tired of their approaches and says, *Lasst ab! Ihr fangt mich nicht!* ("Leave it! You won't get me.") He is after all a knight of the Grail, not formally but intuitively so, being out on this self-selected mission of recapturing the spear that Klingsor stole from Amfortas.

Now Kundry comes along. She too will try to ensnare the hero with her amorous moves. But first she tells him something of her life story, which includes having seen Parsifal as a toddler at his mother's chest. She also tells him how the mother, Herzeleide, tried to shield him from choosing the warrior's way of his father:

[V]or gleicher Not dich zu bewahren,
galt ihr als höchster Pflicht Gebot.
Den Waffen fern, der Männer Kampf und Wüten,
wollte sie still dich bergen und behüten.[40]

Freely translated: "From such miseries she wanted to shield you, that was her plight as a mother, wishing to guard you against weapons and the dangers and sorrows of battle."

Parsifal's mother may have been guided by high ideals in this but as we saw it was of no use: Parsifal intuitively knew that he would be a warrior and he eventually found the warrior's way anyhow. Still, maybe it was good for him to find the way for himself, this nature boy as a champion, the "pure fool" as the one who eventually succeeds in gaining the treasure and save the kingdom.

KUNDRY

Kundry tells Parsifal his name, which he now recalls. Then, when Kundry goes ahead with her seduction and is about to kiss him, Parsifal starts feeling a pain in his heart, being mystically reminded of the wounded Grail king, Amfortas and his wound:

Amfortas!
Die Wunde! Die Wunde! –
Sie brennt in meinem Herzen.[41]

Freely translated: "Amfortas! The wound, the wound! It burns in my heart." The meaning is: Amfortas had been seduced by Kundry, having been enticed by her earthly pleasures. This would seem to be the origin of the wound, according to the original stories; having been injured in "the groin" or "the thigh" could be a code for more elegant

---
[40] Ibid p.23.
[41] Ibid, p.24.

injuries (q. v. Wikipedia/Fisher King). But in the Wagner story only the spear is said to have hurt him. Unclear or not, Amfortas' wound is a symbol telling us that warriors who only fight for earthly rewards are despicable; the true knight fight for honour itself, helping the innocent. That's what a Grail knight should do and that's why the current Grail king, Amfortas is sick: he had let himself be dragged down into the quagmire of materialism.

This shouldn't be interpreted to mean that a hero never should approach a woman; rather, it's a symbolic abbreviation saying that the true hero fights for high ideals, not for money or sex. Curiously, shortly after I had written the first draft of this I read Julius Evola's *The Mystery of the Grail* (1938) where he discusses the ideals of the Grail knights, based on his reading of *Parzifal, Le Morte d'Arthur* and other Arthurian legends. Thus Evola found that chastity indeed was one of the ideals of the Grail knights; however, it was never meant in the form of totally abstaining from women. Because in the Grail legends the knights have many amorous encounters with the women they meet, the respective narrators even stressing that to sleep with a fair woman is good for you. Instead, chastity was about not being led by your carnal desires but by a will to serve and to protect the innocent.

- - -

Parsifal is reminded of the ideals of the Grail knights, of protecting the Grail that contains the blood of Christ; this is the meaning of life for a man, to be a loyal knight, so enough now of fun and games...! He wards off Kundry's approaches. She then confesses her chief sin, having laughed at Christ on the cross. Since then she can only laugh, never cry. But she can be saved too, Parsifal says; it's about willpower, of wishing to be saved. Actually, he doesn't literally say this, instead going on intimating the power of the Grail as the vehicle of salvation, but that's saying the same thing in a symbolic way.

But Kundry doesn't want to be saved. She's not ready for the spiritual life, saying among other things that she won't guide

Parsifal back to the Grail castle. She still tries to tease him into some lovemaking. Parsifal again wards her off: "Away with you, unholy maid!" (*Vergeh, unseliges Weib!*)

THE SPEAR

Now for a masterfully symbolic scene: Kundry, crying for help, summons Klingsor to the chamber. And the villain comes forth, wielding the spear, raising it and saying:

Halt da! Dich bann' ich mit der rechten Wehr!
Den Toren stelle mir seines Meisters Speer![42]

Freely translated: "Halt, you fool, I bind you rightly / with the spear of your master!" – Klingsor throws the spear. But it stops in the air above Parsifal's head; the hero grabs it and holds it high, singing:

Mit diesem Zeichen bann' ich deinen Zauber:
wie die Wunde er schliesse,
die mit ihm du schlugest,
in Trauer und Trümmer
stürz' er die trügende Pracht![43]

Freely translated: "With this sign I bind your curse: / just as it will heal the wound / that you caused him, / in sorrow and rubble / it will topple this vainglory!"

Parsifal makes the sign of the cross with the spear. The castle immediately crumbles, as if by an earthquake, and the rose garden withers. Kundry falls down in a heap, screaming. Parsifal, over the shoulder, says: "You know where you can find me". And curtains.

---

[42] Ibid p.27.
[43] Ibid.

FINAL ACT

Act 2 resolved a lot of things plot wise: we got to know more about Kundry and Parsifal and the latter emerged as a hero. But a lot remains to be resolved: what will become of Kundry and will Parsifal be able to return to the Grail castle and rectify things?

When Act 3 begins many years have passed. Gurnemanz is now a recluse living in a hut outside the Grail castle. On a spring day he finds Kundry lying outside his dwelling. He raises her on her feet, saying that spring is here. When she has gathered herself she starts to serve the holy man like a housemaid. The only word she can say is *Dienen*—serve...! She wants to lead the spiritual life now and eventually she is "saved" by Parsifal: as usual it's expressed in symbols, now by acts of purification and ritual washing.

Then a silent knight comes along, carrying a spear. It takes some time for us to realize that it's Parsifal. The three of them. Kundry, Gurnemanz and Parsifal, have a hard time deciding on what to do, but an atmosphere of quiet joy permeates the scene, underlined by nature waking up from winter's sleep. This tale—whether depending on Wolfram Eschenbach's original or Wagner's poetic abilities—gives us a Christian story with a silvicultural, verdant setting, the presence of the wood making it more relatable for a European than the Bible with its sterile desert lands. Parsifal experiences "the mild soughing of the woods" and the world blossoming due to "the wonders of Good Friday"—*Karfreitagszauber*. Comparing the verdure to that of the rose garden at Klingsor's castle Parsifal sings:

> *Wie dünkt mich doch die Aue heut so schön! –*
> *Wohl traf ich Wunderblumen an,*
> *die bis zum Haupte süchtig mich umrankten;*
> *doch sah ich nie so mild und zart*
> *die Halme, Blüten und Blumen,*
> *noch duftet' all so kindisch hold*
> *und sprach so lieblich traut zu mir.*[44]

---

[44] Ibid p.32.

Freely translated: "How lovely the fields seem to me today! / Indeed I have seen wondrous flowers / reaching out to me with their tendrils; / but never have I seen so mild and tender / herbs, buds and flowers, / smelling so childishly pure / and speaking so lovingly dear to me."

"Good Friday" and "flowery meadow" are two of many leitmotifs in this opera, musically and poetically. The Christian message of compassion and of spirit triumphing over necessity, symbolized in nature's coming to life—this is rather powerful. Rudolf Steiner later had some ideas on this, the scholar like Wagner seeing Christianity in a European light—and in Steiner's case with a thoroughly spiritual, not materialistic founding.

You have to be wary of materialism, even in religious matters. And Steiner in this respect was the man who saw the idea of the Eucharist, of the wine and bread of the Lord's supper actually being transformed into the blood and flesh of Christ, as a wayward materialist idea. The Eucharist is a powerful symbol but not more than a symbol.

HEALING THE WOUND

Nonetheless, the situation at the Grail castle is dire. The old Grail king. Titurel, figuring briefly in Act 1, has died. Why? Because the current Grail king, Amfortas, has stopped serving the Lord's supper to the company. All the knights seem to be feeble and about to die.

The coffin of Titurel is brought forth to be buried. Also carried forth is Amfortas on his stretcher. The sick king laments his father and himself. But then Parsifal steps forth, stretching out the spear and touching Amfortas' wound with it. This, Parsifal says, is the cure for your wound. It's a vague reflection of the sword Notung in *Siegfried*, about which Mime said that only one weapon will do: *Ein Schwert nur taugt zu der Tat* (see chapter 10). And now Parsifal:

Nur eine Waffe taugt:
die Wunde schliesst
der Speer nur, der sie schlug.[45]

---
[45] Ibid p.35.

Freely translated: "Only one weapon suffices: the wound is only healed / by the spear that caused it."

Thus Parsifal has presented himself to the knights; surprised they have witnessed his curative act and now they hear Parsifal continuing to declare the magic powers of the spear. The wound is healed. Next the Grail chalice is uncovered by Parsifal, the choir sings about holy wonder and a light beam illuminates the Grail. And, looking at Parsifal, Kundry falls down lifeless before him, having found redemption. Amfortas and Gurnemanz kneel before Parsifal, the new Grail king, who holds the Grail high in a blessing gesture.

PARSIFAL ON THE MET

I've seen a fine *Parsifal* performance, staged on New York's Metropolitan Opera in March, 2013. It was broadcast on Swedish television on May 25 that year. The show lasted for over five hours and was clearly worth seeing.

Beginning with the stage design it was quite clever, perhaps a little overworked, but all things considered it made an impression. For example I liked this: the giant screen in the background that now showed fleeting clouds, now a large golden circle, now a number of other mysterious forms.

Overall the set design was convincing. The ensemble wore modern clothes, but with style. I know that modern clothes and modern props are anathema to any traditionalistic Wagner lover. I'm often against it too. But not always. For example, this 2013 *Parsifal* production had nothing of the costume-related mess that prevailed in the Bayreuth setting of the same opera in 2012. *Parsifal on the Met* had a sense of direction in its scenography. Modernist, yes, but stylish and with a sense of respect for the story told. (More on the subject of Wagner opera scenography in chapter 19).

As for the singers' effort it was, as far as I can judge, exemplary. The impression was that of a worthy interpretation, faithful to the spirit of Wagner. The ensemble sang in German, as is the norm for Wagner operas. Almost all kinds of opera singers can sing Wagner (Asians, Americans etc.) but in this cast everyone, I gather, were European. This maybe helps when it comes to Wagner, like Englishmen (rather than Americans) are better at playing Shakespeare. For this latter subject, see Al Pacino's documentary *Looking for Richard* from 1996.

In the cast I spotted two Swedes, Peter Mattei as Amfortas and Katarina Dalayman as Kundry. They executed, as far as I can see, their roles excellent. And the German Jonas Kaufmann as Parsifal was a convincing hero, a complex character with traits of both the naive fool and the wilful doer.

The music in this drama is rather discreet and I didn't particularly pay attention to it. But it was there, implicitly and immanently, creating the mood and atmosphere. Conductor was Daniele Gratti.

This production therefore was perfect, as close to perfect as it's possible in a modern framework. I mean, I do prefer a Wagner stage design with traditional, medieval clothing and environments. But you can't have everything. Wagner was a genius and his works are always worthy of seeing, even with some warped scenography. This set was made by people with respect to art, people with the aim to make the work justice. The director, Francois Girard, overall made an impressive work. The backdrop with its shifting images was one of the fortes of this staging, an element showing that modern technology can contribute to the mystery and fantasy feeling of the Wagner operas. Modern Wagner productions aren't all bad, new concepts and ideas in this realm shouldn't always be turned down.

Parsifal in itself is a mysterious play, an enigmatic story that you need to read up on before seeing the opera. With this in mind I'd say that *Parsifal on the Met in 2013* is a great introduction to Wagner.

CONTROVERSY

As we've seen the *Parsifal* story is very much anchored in Christianity. It's about taking the Lord's supper, the beneficial, redeeming qualities of which are stressed again and again in the libretto.

However, it's often intimated that *Parsifal* also is about Aryan blood mystique and such. And Wagner himself thought along those lines. He wrote about it in 1848. And some of these ideas might have found their way into the libretto. Actually, I have a hard time finding these racial and/or pagan ideas in the libretto but at the same time they are indeed to be found in Wagner's writings.

According to Lundewall Wagner in the 1840's was trying to re-interpret the Grail complex into something pagan. Lundewall doesn't mention Wagner's sources but as a side-note there is a European tradition for this, in later times represented by the above mentioned Evola and *The Mystery of the Grail*. Wagner's ideas are given in a prose draft called *Die Wibelungen* (*The Wibelung*) from 1848, a sort of epilogue to The Ring. In this draft the treasure of the Nibelung in time is said to have morphed into the Grail, which in the old scriptures isn't a chalice but a stone. Lundewall relates the perspective of neither the Grail nor the spear having anything to do with Christian legend. The weapon, for its part, in this respect is the spear of Wotan having become whole again.

The spear and the Grail were preserved in Montsalvat by knights, being direct descendants to Siegfried the dragon-slayer. This detail is mirrored in *Parsifal* with presenting the bow-equipped youngster in Act 1 with a leitmotif that's related to the Siegfried motif.

HEROISM AND CHRISTIANITY

Lundewall tells us that the speculations of the Wibelungen text were continued by Wagner in another essay, "Heldentum und Christentum" ("Heroism and Christianity"), published in Bayreuther Blätter 1878. There it's said: the early medieval German chieftains, and later on the German emperors of the Holy Roman empire, had their origins in the above mentioned Grail knights. Their battles in the east were like fighting the dragon on another level. Wagner for one saw it as a battle against creatures of a lower standing order. And this battle is also to be fought at home, with people imagining that they stem from monkeys (Darwinists), in conflict against men who know they are descendants of gods. The godly people have racial consciousness, the lowlifes haven't; they are materialistic trash people trying to drag down the race of gods into decay and misery.

According to Wagner the Grail knights had this philosophy. And Amfortas of the medieval *Parzival* story has committed miscegenation with Kundry, thus debasing himself and the knights, and thus receiving a wound that won't heal.

Also, Lundewall intimates, Wagner being a vegetarian was against "consuming the flesh and blood of Christ". Thus the Lord's supper would have to be re-interpreted, maybe along the above sketched, pagan lines.

Thus Wagner according to Lundewall's summary. From other sources we have it that Hitler savoured Wagner's ideas in this respect, seeing *Parsifal* as something of a Germanic blood myth. An indication is given here, in an article in UK's The Telegraph on July 25, 2011, "Hitler and Wagner".[46]

No source is given for the Hitler quote delivered below. That said, for what it's worth I hereby give you The Telegraph's take on the specific subject I've been discussing:

> Hitler reinterpreted the story of Wagner's final opera Parsifal to fit his own ideological vision. The story carries elements of Buddhist renunciation suggested by Wagner's readings of Schopenhauer. However, Hitler wrote of it: "What is celebrated is not the Christian Schopenhauerian [sic] religion of compassion, but pure and noble blood, blood whose purity the brotherhood of initiates has come together to guard."

As I said, no source is given for the Hitler quote. However, that Hitler had some interest in *Parsifal*, this we also see in Joachim Fest's Hitler biography from 1973. In 1935, returning by train from the re-militarized Rhine land and travelling through the nocturnal Ruhr area

---

[46] http://www.telegraph.co.uk/culture/music/classicalmusic/8659814/Hitler-and-Wagner.html

Hitler wanted to hear music, and meditating to the *Parsifal* overture he said: "On Parsifal I build my religion, a solemn worship without theatrical humility. Only in a hero's outfit you can serve God."[47]

So where am I heading with all this? Overall, I think, there's a reason in discussing this since some Wagner lovers of today tend to silence and cover up the controversial sides of their idol. As intimated above the *Parsifal* libretto is not so suspect in itself, catering to the common form of Christianity since late antiquity, both Catholic and Protestant: take the Lord's supper and be free, because the Grail contains the blood of Christ and the wine of the Eucharist *is* his blood. However, Wagner the writer had his private ideas of the meaning of the Grail, the spear and the knights that guard it. And in those ideas there are elements of racialism and purity of blood, ideas reportedly adopted by Hitler.

---

[47] Hitler quoted after the Swedish edition, 1974, of Fest's biography, p .568; translated by the author. Specifically, Fest seems to have gotten the Hitler quote from Hans Frank, Im Angesicht des Galgens, 1955.

12. WAGNER AND NIETZSCHE

Wagner's relation to Friedrich Nietzsche is a fascinating narrative in the history of Western culture. Being something of a syncretist I admire them both, being led by both the beauty of Wagner's music and the symbolism of *Thus Spake Zarathustra*. The subject of Wagner and Nietzsche collects many threads—music, philosophy, "being German" (versus being Anglo-American or Latin European)—but here I'll focus on Nietzsche's opinions on Wagner's music. The criticism carried weight but should not be seen as the death knell of Wagner's art, as some tend to do.

VILLA TRIEBSCHEN

How did Wagner's friendship with Nietzsche begin? According to Mayer the two of them first met in Leipzig, November 1868, at the house of professor Hermann Brockhaus. Wagner by then reportedly was an admirer of Nietzsche. And Nietzsche was captivated by Wagner's music. Nietzsche was 30 years Wagner's junior, born in 1844 and thus 24 by this time, only at the beginning of his career as philosopher. But as intimated he seems to have made some impression on his surroundings having gotten Wagner's attention.

The next year Nietzsche was invited to Wagner and his wife Cosima in Switzerland, Villa Triebschen in Lucerne. Nietzsche himself by then lived in the same land as professor in Basel. In 1870

Nietzsche was present at the first performance of Wagner's piano piece "Siegfried Idyl", on Cosima's birthday on December 25th in the Lucerne villa.

By this companionship Nietzsche seems to have been won for the Wagner cause, as a prophet for all things Wagnerian. The textual evidence is the essay *Richard Wagner in Bayreuth*, part of Nietzsche's *Untimely Observations* from 1875-76. In this essay Nietzsche among other things praises the folksy, "populist" character of Wagner's music. Wagner himself may have influenced these thoughts. Because, eventually, in the overall reception the Wagner operas didn't become a new kind of folk art, instead becoming more of a bourgeois art (more on this in chapter 22). But to understand the Nietzsche-Wagner relationship we first have to see what Nietzsche says about the folksy element of the operas in question:

> If there's anything that sets his [Wagner's] art apart from all other art in recent times, it's this: it doesn't any longer speak the learned language of a cast, nor by any means does it know the opposition between learned and unlearned... The existence of an art shining brightly and warmly like the sun, illuminating the poor in spirit as well as melting the pride of the learned, this was something that was impossible to figure out by guessing, it had to be experienced.[48]

This was a pipe-dream. Wagner operas today are a matter for the bourgeoisie, not for the people. Then again: any modern film lover knows that Wagner wrote the "Ride of the Valkyries" and that this piece accompanies a scene in Coppola's *Apocalypse Now* (1979). What other opera melody can claim such a fame in the 21st century? What other opera composer does the man in the street know except for Wagner?

Nietzsche sought the folksy element in Wagner's art. He hoped for a new art, an art appealing to the masses. Wagner did so too. Even when Bayreuth was completed and the composer saw it becoming a haunt for the bourgeoisie and the aristocracy, that it hadn't become

---

[48] Nietzsche quoted after Mayer, p.165; translated by the author.

a place of pilgrimage for the people, high and low, united like never before by his music; when this didn't happen Wagner for one didn't scrap his project. No, he kept staging his operas there, he himself presiding in this the temple of his art, receiving artists, celebrities, aristocrats and monarchs such as the kaiser, the emperor of Brazil and the king of Württemberg.

BAYREUTH

Nietzsche saw all this, being present in Bayreuth at the 1876 première. Mayer says that Nietzsche's friendship with Wagner and Cosima somehow got left behind in Villa Triebschen. For when visiting the pair in their German dwelling in 1876, their Bayreuth house, Villa Wahnfried, an interesting incident occurred: Nietzsche put the "Triumphlied" by Brahms on the music stand of the grand piano. Angrily Wagner threw it aside. Mayer scolds Wagner for this kind of reaction, for being the priest of his own cult intimating "ye shall have no other gods before me"... Brahms, Handel, Medelssohn and Schumann were prohibited in Wagner's household. But I'd say: if an artist has an obsession like this you have to accept it. And an artist disliking his contemporary rivals is rather the rule than the exception, I'd say.

Nietzsche putting sheet music by Brahms on the piano was the act of a jester provoking a reaction, not someone trying to please a friend. The philosopher soon left Bayreuth, disappointed. In fact, he seems to have entered in a state of depression after this; the break with Wagner affecting him deeply.

Nietzsche's despondency had other reasons than this breakup, like having to quit the position as professor in Basel for health reasons. But eventually he bounced back, living on a pension from the university and being able to write what he wished. In fact he wrote about one book per year during the 1880's and in 1888 he wrote five. One of these was the scathing *The Case of Wagner* (*Der Fall Wagner*, 1888). Here the philosopher said: Wagner is the consummate rhetorician, his music "means" this and that. His music is merely an instrument, an illustration of stories and ideas. The rhetorical feature generates a false, seductive music.

THE CASE OF WAGNER

This Nietzsche meant now. And he was more or less correct in his assessment. I mean, Wagner remains a classic and now he's more performed than ever. But his aesthetics has its faults and Nietzsche was among the first to note them.

In his 1888 critique Nietzsche continues: Wagner strikes poses and makes gestures. Also, the music becomes dark with the Wotan passion, "the bad weather god". And the eternal "speech-song" and the *endless melody* make the works heavy and cumbersome, not light and witty as the southern operas à la Bizet.

This also was a rather well-founded criticism. However, Nietzsche wasn't a hater of all things Wagnerian. In the same year (1888), Nietzsche in *Ecce Homo* for example praised the Wagner who created *Tristan and Isolde*. The Tristan music was modern, it was true, it said something real in a new way, Nietzsche seems to mean. His views may symbolize the general acclaim for this opera which since has only grown. Tristan musically was Wagner's artistic triumph and epitome; then Wagner created The Ring and *Die Meistersinger* and they, Nietzsche thought, weren't as advanced. And with this you can agree. However, I don't discard The Ring altogether as Nietzsche does.

Hereby the quote from *Ecce Homo*, the chapter "Warum ich so Klug bin", 6th Division, where Nietzsche celebrates Wagner's Tristan[49]:

> From the moment you could get a piano score of Tristan (...) I was a Wagnerian. The earlier works of Wagner I thought nothing of — still too common, too "German"... However, still I search for a work of equally dangerous fascination, of equally sweet and fearsome

---

[49] English translation by the author.

infinity as that of Tristan—I search in vain in all the arts. All the grotesqueries of Leonardo da Vinci lose their magic at the first note of Tristan. This work is absolutely Wagner's non plus ultra; he recuperated from it with the Meistersinger and the Ring. (...) I consider myself lucky having lived at the right time and having lived precisely among Germans, so as to be ripe for this work: my psychologist's curiosity goes that far. The world is poor for one who has never been sick enough for this "voluptuousness of hell": it is permissible, it is almost imperative to employ a mystic formula here. I think I know better than anyone else the enormities Wagner was capable of, the fifty worlds of strange ecstasies, for which no one outside of him had the wingspan; and such as I am, strong enough to turn even the most questionable and dangerous things to my advantage and become stronger thereby, I call Wagner the great benefactor of my life.

Here it's also interesting to note Nietzsche's affirmation of being German. Earlier he had, for instance, meant that Wagner's championing of "German culture" was a contradiction in terms.[50]

PUT IN PERSPECTIVE

Nietzsche overall criticised Wagner but his views were rather sound. True, this attack had some yellow journalism-approach to it, with Nietzsche's tone in *The Case of Wagner* being spiteful and sarcastic. But as we've seen he could also (in *Ecce Homo*) cut the man, Wagner, some slack. Indeed praise him, even in 1888.

Nietzsche's criticism didn't kill Wagner's oeuvre, as some may think. If I may put up a straw-man it would be something like this, some may have this image of it: "First Wagner triumphed. Then Nietzsche came and said it was all bluff. From then on no one could in earnest like Wagner's music. End of story." But art criticism doesn't

---

[50] Source Wikipedia, entry Friedrich Nietzsche.

work that way. Nietzsche's words carried weight but he didn't stop Wagner operas from being performed. The Wagner opus lived on and it still lives on.

Wagner's operas suffered some damage from Nietzsche's attack but they lived on as an art work, as a holistic phenomenon, as an *oeuvre*. And Nietzsche's criticism is now a part of that *oeuvre*. This is a lesson on how the *reception* of a work becomes a virtually integral part of the work. No Wagner historian can ignore the concept "Friedrich Nietzsche" when he depicts the life and work of the composer. Nietzsche and Wagner are united forever in a hate-love relationship, a virtual embrace of the philosopher both admiring and hating the composer. As we've seen Nietzsche in 1876 wrote the panegyric *Richard Wagner in Bayreuth*. It's rather heavy in style and predictable in content (Wagner is the archetypal genius) but at the same time it can't be ignored from the view of the Wagner reception. In this paper we see Wagner depicted in the role of artist-as-magician. Wagner indeed had this talent, of becoming swept away like a shaman on an astral trip. Maybe he got too carried away sometimes but the genius that Nietzsche also saw, this still lives on—on opera stages world wide, in spite of the faults of the Wagner operas. You have to be able to unite both the good and not so good aspects of the work in order to enjoy it, I think.

The role of Wagner as a magician for its part is captured by Ingvar Lundewall in his bio *Trollkarlen från Bayreuth* (1989). Having sketched the philosophy, characters and diverse plot moves of The Ring Lundewall states this, a kind of summary uniting everything that can be said concerning a massive work of art like The Ring, and why not the whole Wagner *oeuvre*. I've quoted it before and now I do it again:

> Ideas, theories and analyses whether *Der Ring des Nibelungen* is a problem play or a political or aesthetic revolution drama, a logically rigorous antique tragedy or a mosaic pattern, a romantic fairytale drama, an opera or a "music drama"—all alternative interpretations lose every sense in the dark of the opera salon, as

soon as Wagner the Shaman exerts his magic on stage and in the orchestral pit.[51]

---

[51] p.134; translated by the author.

13. ON WAGNER IN D'ANNUNZIO'S *THE FLAME OF LIFE*

he Wagnerian art has a mighty hold on people. Even on those who say that they don't like him. Hereby a memorable example of this.

Gabriele d'Annunzio (1863-1938) was an Italian writer, poet and playwright in the traditional vein. He praised the Roman antiquity, the renaissance and the *Risorgimento* era of renewed Italian grandeur in the realms of art and politics. Later on he became a politician and a soldier. But up until 1900 he was more focused on art, culture and the charms of being a private citizen. For instance, in his 1900 novel *The Flame of Life* (*Il Fuoco*) he discussed art and creativity, while at the same time telling a love story and painting a portrait of the city where it all plays, Venice.

The novel begins in the autumn of 1882. The poet, playwright and composer Stelio Effrena is going by gondola to the Palazzo Ducale in order to deliver a speech on traditional art and the artist as a transcendentally gifted seer. He is accompanied by his amour, the actress La Foscarina, who on the way points to things she thinks will inspire him. She is Stelio's muse. The novel truly lives and breathes art and the artist way of life.

Having delivered his speech in the palace, Stelio and La Foscarina attends a dinner with some friends. And at the table they discuss art. Specifically, they talk about the performing arts. A certain Daniele Glauro delves into essential things like *rite* and *cult*, stating that the drama is to be a church service and a sermon. Theatre performances, he means, must again become solemn as a rite. On stage we have the preacher-actor revealing the word, with the audience playing the role of the attentively listening congregation.

GIANCOLO

But this is Bayreuth, a certain prince Hoditz interposes. No, says Stelio, the hero of the novel and d'Annunzio's alter ego, it's Giancolo, a Roman hill where the Italians will build a similar temple in praise of Italian opera and Mediterranean classic culture. Stelio seems to have only contempt for Bayreuth, being only a house of brick and wood. Their own temple will be in marble. And when someone asks Stelio if he verily is no admirer of Wagner, he says:

> Richard Wagner's work (...) is an expression of the Germanic spirit, being essentially and entirely a child of the North. His reformation is akin to Luther's. His work represents the finest flower of his own people's culture, the quintessence of all the efforts having been made by the German musicians and poets, from Bach to Beethoven, from Wieland to Goethe. If you try to imagine his work placed on the Mediterranean beaches, among our bright olive trees and our laurels here in the clear light of the Latin heavens, you would see how it faded away and dissolved into a naught. Wagner himself says that it's the artist's mission to bring to perfection a yet unformed world, the artist desiring and hoping to enjoy it before it's even created. And that's exactly what I do when I proclaim a new or renewed art—and art which, with its strong and clear simplicity, with its energetic grace, with its warmth and its harmonic purity, continues to crown the mighty works that our chosen people have built. I'm proud of being Latin and—forgive me, lady Myrta and Hoditz!—to me, each of a different blood is a barbarian.[52]

---

[52] p.97, quoted from the Swedish version of Il Fuoco, entitled Elden; translated by

In the company we then have a certain Baldassare Stampa, having recently visited Bayreuth and become a staunch Wagnerian. He says that even Wagner was classically trained, he knew about ancient Greek culture. Stelio admits that but means that Wagner's ideas are confused, saying that it's hard to imagine anything more different from the Orestes drama than The Ring of the Nibelung. Stelio's heart and soul is with the southern cultural style, from antiquity over the Renaissance up until present day. There is also mentioned the Italian reformer Emilio del Cavalliere who had reshaped the opera salon according to the same ideas as Wagner, *mutatis mutandum*.

MONTEVERDI

The company then seems to agree on the fact that Claudio Monteverdi (1567-1643) was the greatest opera composer ever. This creator of the opera genre proper is called "divine" in the novel, "a great spirit of the noblest Italian blood". Elements of Monteverdi's operas are quoted and sung by the company, and by this Stelio Effrena seems to have proved that Italian opera symbolized by Monteverdi is rather superior to Wagner.

But the argument isn't over yet. Baldassare, the Wagner lover, has an ace card in the form of *Parsifal*: what about the lament of the sick king, Amfortas, isn't that something? But this, says Stelio, is surpassed in a Palestrina motet, older, more pure and forceful than Wagner.

Then the Wagner fan keeps on stressing the genius of *Parsifal*, of the loving struggle between Kundry and Parsifal in Klingsor's castle, and this reminds Stelio of his love for his companion La Foscarina, the actress who joins him at the table.

Baldassare keeps on praising scenes from *Parsifal*, and to this Stelio has no answer:

the author.

Stelio Effrena fell silent. He felt like being crushed under the weight of the mighty works of the German barbarian. [But then he also sees a kindred spirit in Wagner; the both of them, Stelio and the German, are geniuses creating great works of art. The German [...] had succeeded in enthusing a whole world with his personality and his art. In order to win a victory over men and things he had done the same as he himself had done: having been completely engulfed in his fantasy world, fashioning his own, all-encompassing dream of beauty. Even he had sought out his audience like looking for a desirable pray, setting up as his life's goal to always surpass himself. And now he *did* have a temple dedicated to the cult of himself, up there among the Bavarian mountains...[53]

Art alone is able to bring people together, Daniele Glauro then interposes, while Stelio continues his reveries. Glauro continues:

Let us therefore honour the great master who forever has pledged art his allegiance! His *Festspielhaus* may be built of wood and brick, it may be narrow and imperfect—but let's not forget that it's filled with a sublime content! For there is revealed art as religion, as embodied in a living form. The drama is a temple service.

And so the company unanimously praises Richard Wagner.

THE MASTERPIECE

Stelio, having become silent after all this praising of Wagner, in the mean time experiences a mental struggle: the fire of creativity flames inside this artist set to create The Masterpiece. Then the company discusses the nationalist element of Wagner's art and Stelio privately and silently acknowledges this, musing on how Wagner's works express the grandeur of the German people from medieval times up until the victories over the Austrians and the French at Sadowa and Sedan:

---

[53] Ibid p.105.

The same victory had crowned the work of the sword and the art. Like the hero the poet had completed a work of liberation. Like the blood of the Iron Chancellor and the blood of the soldiers even his musical creations had contributed to the glorification and persistence of the people.[54]

Right after Stelio has made this reflection prince Hoditz remarks that Wagner actually lives in the selfsame city, Venice, at this point of time, in Palazzo Vendramin-Calergi. Then everyone can see the composer for their inner eye, small in physical stature but with such grandeur in the posture that he becomes something of a demigod, born by the eternal youth of the Siegfried character. And Stelio, who began by reducing Wagner into nothing special, now acknowledges how the Wagner myth has him in its power, only slightly diminished when prince Hoditz says that Wagner now is very tired and fragile, he's heartsick, otherwise he would have attended the event in the Palazzo Ducale which this chapter is about.

WAGNER DOWNTOWN

Later in the novel Stelio and his woman spots Wagner downtown, in the distance: old and grey but still exuding the magic of the master. This even happens twice. And in the final section of the novel, taking place half a year later, in February 1883, they receive the message that Wagner has just passed away. Stelio and his artist friends then ask the widow if they can be given the honour to carry the coffin to the train station, where the remains are to be transported for the burial in Villa Wahnfried in Bayreuth. This is granted to them.

Thus the Wagner presence is marked throughout the novel. The novel is rather long and the Wagner theme is but a sub-theme, but nonetheless. Stelio/d'Annunzio affirms the supremacy of his Italian culture but he also bows to Wagner as a representative of The Genial Artist. As intimated Stelio sees Wagner as a kindred spirit: the

---

[54] p.111.

artist who, elevated in a trance, goes to unseen lands and afterwards envisions it, portraying it in his works of art.

Thus d'Annunzio in *The Flame of Life* gives a rather profound image of how an Italian, steeped in Monteverdi operas and antique culture, being wary of the northernness and a bit cumbersome character of Wagner's operas, at the same time affirms the sheer power and mystique of the Wagner *oeuvre*. This artist's view of the artist Wagner to me is more honest than the philosopher's view on the same subject, that of how Nietzsche viewed Wagner. Even Nietzsche could, as seen in the previous chapter, confess that Wagner was complex but d'Annunzio's Wagner vision in this respect is more variegated and encompassing.

And why is this? It's by being an artistic vision—by being the sub-theme of a novel—and by not being a dissertation, like Nietzsche's *Der Fall Wagner*.

14. ON COMPOSING DRAMAS ABOUT SAINTS

Wagner once was planning to do an opera about Buddha: *The Victors* (*Die Sieger*). The prose draft and musical sketches for this is dated 1856 in Wagner's "List of Works for the Stage" on Wikipedia. But the project came to naught. Thomas Mann in *Wagner und unsere Zeit* has found the answer in a Wagner letter from 1858, where the composer realizes how hard it is to make a dramatic and musical exposition of a man elevated above all passions. The holy, thoroughly pacified is artistically lifeless. Holiness and drama doesn't go easily together.

The same could be said about Wagner's plans for a Jesus opera: *Jesus von Nazareth*. This only materialized as a prose draft, written in 1848-49. Now of course you *can* dramatize the saintly life. Art and holiness sometimes do meet...! As for Buddha we've had Hesse's novel *Siddharta* (1922). The four gospels for their part tell an exciting story; this isn't just about Jesus preaching, they also tell us about parts of his life. I know of no memorable Jesus novel but we've had several Jesus movies. And we even have a musical drama: *Jesus Christ Superstar* (1970). Was this the Jesus opera that Wagner never made...?

I won't speculate about Andrew Lloyd Webber having the ambition to fulfil Wagner's dream of a Jesus opera. But looking at the Webber work on this subject can tell us a bit about the process of taking a historical-mythical subject and making it into a stage production that people can relate to. Overall the Wagner art didn't become "the art of the future" (as he himself may have thought at the time) but the Wagner approach to staging a story musically is still viable. Wagner, to me, rises above the rest of 19th century opera composers and *Jesus Christ Superstar* rises above the rest of 20th century musicals. Why? Because of the spiritual message. Most late 19th century operas are about ordinary people in everyday situations and the same goes for the random musical. But Jesus Christ Superstar has a modicum of spirituality and this sets it apart.

Not that Webber, and his librettist Tim Rice, set out to do a *Parsifal*. It was a pop musical about a hippie Jesus. That said, overall I think they made the subject justice. I mean, the Jesus we meet in this work isn't the epitome of mysticism. He's something of an indulger. But Rice/Webber didn't go all the way into nihilism.

Also, they made the love story element work, if only hinted at. It's with having Mary Magdalene in a central role. And in having Jesus and Mary sing a love duet it becomes somewhat Wagnerian. I mean, as we know when "boy meets girl" in Wagner's operas, when a man and a woman occupies the stage they always fall in love. The idea of Jesus and Mary as a loving couple gets a slight syrupy treatment in *Jesus Christ Superstar* with the song "Could We Start Again, Please?" from Act 2. This used to be my least favourite song of the show. But the theory of a Jesus-Mary-love affair is indeed supported by a Gnostic gospel, the Gospel of Philip, telling us how Jesus loved Mary more than all the disciples and used to kiss her on the mouth. Then the apostles asked, "Why do you love her more than all of us?" Jesus then answered and said to them, "Why do I not love you like her?"

Not much of this is found in the musical. But the spirit of it is caught in intimations such as the duet, see above, a duet that I now appreciate from an operatic point of view. And so, unscientifically I say: if Wagner had done a Jesus opera he might have put in some kind of operatic expression of love between Jesus and Mary Magdalene. And the rest of the Rice-Webber musical could give indications of how the rest would have looked. However, Wagner might have added a scene of the resurrection though, this logical end curiously absent from Rice-Webber's Jesus story. I mean, Jesus clad in white coming out of the grave on the third day, how fitting for an opera scene isn't that...?

15. ON BEING CONTROVERSIAL

Wagner is controversial. You just can't deny it. Only an insular mind, let's say, a music-lover seduced by Wagner's artistic powers, would try to white-wash Wagner into "just another composer". He is not and never will be, and this because of his socio-political views. I mean, it still is possible to enjoy Wagner's music without every time having to conjure up images of Hitler and World War II. The Tristan chord, Lohegrin marrying Elsa, Senta's Ballade—this has absolutely nothing to do with the Third Reich. But at the same time, as a historian pondering what Wagner and his *oeuvre* overall represents, it's impossible not to go into the controversial aspects. Not doing it would underline them. So even as a Wagner fan you have to grasp the nettle in this respect, admitting that he was and always will be a subject of controversy.

A PAMPHLET

In 1850 Wagner published an essay in Neue Zeitschrift für Musik. He used the pseudonym K. Freigedank ("K. Freethought"). The text was later published separately as a pamphlet, in expanded form and under Wagner's real name, in 1869. The title was "Das Judenthum in der Musik" ("Jewishness in Music").[55] In the 1850 article Wagner

---

[55] I base this summary on Wikipedia, on the entries "Das Judenthum in der Musik" and "Wagner controversies".

denounces Jewish music completely. The music of a Jewish composer such as Mendelsohn, Wagner says, is charming but without depth. Another Jewish composer, Meyerbeer (1791-1864), popular in Wagner's day and still alive in 1850, is fiercely attacked but not named. The general tenor of the essay is belligerent and antagonistic.

That's the reality of Wagner's anti-Semitic thought. The ignoble character of it is underlined by this: he attacks Meyerbeer, the self-same composer who helped him while in Paris to have the Dresden opera to stage *Rienzi*. According to Wikipedia[56] Meyerbeer wrote to its director, saying that *Rienzi* was "rich in fantasy and of great dramatic effect." Meyerbeer also endorsed *The Flying Dutchman*.

Wagner had a hang-up about Giacomo Meyerbeer. This German composer had succeeded in breaking in Paris with operas like *Robert le diable* and *Les Hugenots* and Wagner seems to never have come over this. In his memoir (*Mein Leben*, 1870) Wagner notes how glad he is at the news of Meyerbeer's death. It's at the end of the book; in 1864 Wagner has just been contacted by Bavaria's king Ludwig with the promise of friendship and financial support and thus Wagner's has triumphed career-wise; he can look forward to stagings of his operas on a grander, more systematic scale than before. And then he and his company hear of Meyerbeer's death:

> While we were at table Eckert was informed by telegram of Meyerbeer's death in Paris, and Weisheimer burst out in boorish laughter to think that the master of opera, who had done me so much harm, had by a strange coincidence not lived to see this day.[57]

Clearly, this is Wagner at his worst.

About the anti-Semitism of Wagner a lot can be said. For instance, in his defence it's said that he worked with Jewish conductors, like Hermann Levi who conducted the première of

---

[56] Entry: Rienzi.
[57] Quoted from the English translation published in New York, 1911, as seen in online form on Project Gutenberg.org: http://www.gutenberg.org/cache/epub/5144/pg5144.html

Parsifal in Bayreuth, 1882. Okay. And the accusations that the villains of his operas—Mime, Klingsor, Beckmesser—are Jewish caricatures are vague. At least there's nothing in the libretti in question that portrays them as Jewish. Mime for his part is a capitalist, Klingsor is an upstart devoid of spirituality and Beckmesser is a pedant, alien to the true spirit of art. And there's nothing specifically Jewish about all this. We find the Mimes, Klingsors and Beckmessers in our midst, irrespective of nationality.

That said, the opinions in the 1850 essay were Wagner's and he held them all his life. Liszt, Brahms, Beethoven etc. never wrote about "Jewishness in music" but Wagner did. Wagner wasn't an anti-Semite through and through but he did hold some anti-Semitic views.

CHAUVINISM

"Chauvinism" usually translates as "excessive feelings of grandeur", mostly of the nationalist kind. As the keen reader of this book has noted I'm no enemy of nationalism per se. For instance, in the 19th century it was legit for a German to strive for some kind of unification of the diverse lands, duchies and cities of Germany. The early 19th century for its part had seen French occupation of Germany, a time of humiliation, possible only because of German fragmentation and disunion. The Prussian variety of German nationalism that ensued after 1871 normally is seen as a turn for the worse but I don't share that view. Wagner's nationalism mostly was the definition of decency.

I say, mostly. Wagner namely also succumbed to chauvinist feelings. After the Franco-Prussian war, after the main battles had been fought and the Prussian army had taken Paris, in January 1871, Wagner composed a poem called, "To the German Army Before Paris" ("An das deutsche Heer vor Paris"). According to Mayer it advocates the total annexation of France (that is, intimating that Germany should not be satisfied with the annexation of the partly German speaking lands of Lothringia and Elsass). At the same time (written in 1870, published in 1873) we have Wagner's short play

"A Capitulation" ("Eine Kapitulation"), a parody that tells us of the inferiority of French art. In the play Germans are scolded only for admiring this artistic style. In particular Victor Hugo is lambasted as the evil genius of realism. Now, artistic freedom aside—an artist should be allowed to write anything—the context of which this play is part, that of Germany having recently conquered France, makes it into a display of Wagner's tendency to display chauvinist feelings.

A POLITICIAN

Germany's political leader 1933-45 was Adolf Hitler (1889-1945). In today's discussion—this is written in 2014—Hitler seems to be the very definition of controversy. And German scholar Joachim Fest (see below) used to say that Hitler's world view was thoroughly shaped by Wagner.

This is a statement worthy of discussion, Hitler being decisively shaped by Wagner. As an artist—Wagner—this is as far as you can get in being controversial. But for now and as a starting point, let's focus on the mere fact that Hitler the private person liked Wagner. This is common knowledge. For instance, in his memoir *Mein Kampf* Hitler mentions a Wagner experience when he was 12, attending the theatre in Linz. There he saw the first opera of his life...

> ... *Lohengrin*. I was captivated at once. My youthful enthusiasm for the master of Bayreuth knew no bounds. Again and again I was drawn to his works and today I consider it particularly fortunate that the modesty of that provincial performance reserved for me the opportunity of seeing increasingly better productions.[58]

---

[58] Chapter 1, "At Home", from the English 1941 version My Struggle, as seen online on Internet Archive; German original 1926: https://archive.org/stream/meinkampf035176mbp/meinkampf035176mbp_djvu.txt

RICHARD WAGNER — A PORTRAIT

Hitler's favourite Wagner opera is said to have been *The Master-Singers of Nuremberg*. *Parsifal* also had its power over him (see chapter 11). Wikipedia[59] says that...

> ...Hitler was a fanatical admirer of Wagner's music, and sought to incorporate it into his heroic mythology of the German nation. Hitler held many of Wagner's original scores in his Berlin bunker at the end of World War II, despite the pleadings of Wieland Wagner to have these important documents put in his care; the scores perished with Hitler in the final days of the war.

These facts seem legit. With Richard Evans as the source (*The Coming of the Third Reich,* 2004) Wikipedia[60] then has this to say:

> After Wagner's death in 1883, Bayreuth increasingly became a focus for German nationalists attracted by the mythos of the operas, who have been referred to by latter commentators as the Bayreuth Circle. This group was endorsed by Cosima Wagner, whose anti-Semitism was considerably less complex and more virulent than Richard's. One of the circle was Houston Stewart Chamberlain, the author of a number of 'philosophic' tracts which later became required Nazi reading. Chamberlain married Wagner's daughter, Eva.

Richard Wagner had a son named Siegfried (1869-1930). Siegfried had an English-born wife, Winifred. After the deaths of Siegfried and Cosima in 1930 Winifred became the leading figure at Bayreuth. Wikipedia has this on her relationship to Hitler[61]:

> In 1923, Winifred met Adolf Hitler, who greatly admired Wagner's music. (...) Although Winifred remained personally faithful to Hitler, she denied that she had ever supported the Nazi party.

---

[59] Entry: Wagner Controversies.
[60] Ibid.
[61] Entry: Winifred Wagner.

Her relationship with Hitler grew so close that by 1933 there were rumours of impending marriage. Haus Wahnfried, the Wagner home in Bayreuth, became Hitler's favourite retreat. Hitler gave the festival government assistance and tax exempt status, and treated Winifred's children solicitously.

This is also common knowledge. Hitler was welcome at Bayreuth and Villa Wahnfried. All the above gives the Wagner heritage some controversial colouring.

JOACHIM FEST

Stated more to the point: was Richard Wagner the spiritual father of Adolf Hitler and Nazism? One man seems to mean that: Joachim Fest (1926-2006).

Fest was a German historian and something of a Hitler expert. His Hitler biography from 1973 has 950 pages in the Swedish edition. (Below I will quote from this edition, issued by Berghs in 1974; the name of the original was *Hitler—Eine Biographie*.) Fest makes some bold statements and sometimes he goes too far, but he certainly has a point in saying that Hitler was influenced by Wagner, not solely music-wise, but as a role-model of The Artist and as a right-winger.

In the early 20th century the 16 year old Hitler was living in the Austrian province town of Linz, with his mother subsiding on a pension granted them after the death of Hitler's father in 1903. Hitler is often said to have visited the opera. Fest tells us how enchanted Hitler was by seeing the opera *Rienzi*, about the 14th century Roman rebel. Now we come to a disputed eye-witness, Hitler's friend August Kubizek. In 1953 Kubizek issued the memoir *Adolf Hitler, mein Jugenfreund* (*Adolf Hitler, My Youth-hood Friend*). This is the source when Fest tells us how, after a performance of *Rienzi*, Hitler had taken Kubizek up on a hill called Freinberg. With the darkened city of Linz below them Hitler had begun speaking, his words bursting forth from him like flood waters. In reportedly grandiose, inspiring pictures Hitler envisioned his own future and that of his people. Later, in 1939, the two friends met in Bayreuth, Kubizek having been invited by the then Reichskanzler. And when Kubizek reminded his friend about that night on the hill outside Freinberg, Hitler vividly recalled it, concluding: "In that hour it began."

Now, we only have Kubizeks version of this. So okay, this story can be doubted. Then again, Kubizek was no novelist or dramatic artist, he was just writing a memoir. So the episode could be true.

In 1907 Hitler moved to the Austrian capital, Vienna. In this milieu, pre-war Vienna, Wagner was very much *en vogue* and his operas were regularly performed, so in the mind of Fest the process of Wagner forming the young Hitler continued unabated. Apart from enjoying the music Hitler admired Wagner the artist, the composer like no one else impersonating the artistic lifestyle. With Hermann Rauschning (*Gespräche mit Hitler,* 1940) as source, Fest tells us that Hitler said that except for Wagner he didn't have any precursors, referring to Wagner's role as a personality and a prophet of the German people. Hitler admired the courage and energy of Wagner, having also been highly excited when he realized his affinity with the great composer.

SIMILARITIES

Hitler saw himself and Wagner as two of a kind. They were similar. So which were those similarities? In what way did Hitler identify with Wagner? According to Fest they were both artists, Hitler not being so successful as such but he had talent as a draughtsman and knew something about art as a phenomenon and as a livelihood. Secondly both had encountered adversities in life but had overcome them, Wagner as a composer, Hitler as a politician. Thirdly, both were vegetarians.

Then there was the role of the outsider, depicted in some Wagner operas, how a rebel challenges the current order of things. Fest:

> In *Rienzi* or *Lohengrin*, *Stolzing* or *Tannhäuser* Hitler in an elevated form recognized his own enmity towards the world, and sometimes it seems that he has tried to copy his paragon in a direct way. Both had the will to power and a basically despotic tendency. The art of Richard Wagner highly shows it being the instrument of an unbending, far-reaching will to command.[62]

Fest's approach to the subject is somewhat excessive, as we see in this quote, but I give him the benefit of my doubt. Clearly there are more than superficial similarities between Hitler and Wagner.

Fest goes on to summarize how Hitler was influenced by Wagner the polemicist. Hitler read his pamphlets, Fest says without any source to support it (and Richard Evans in *The Third Reich in Power,* 2005, says that there is no evidence that Hitler ever read any of Wagner's writings). But okay, this Hitler reportedly got from Wagner: the anti-Semitism, the idea of German supremacy and the blood mysticism of *Parsifal* (Wagner had some "pagan" ideas on this, see chapter 11). More loosely Fest says that Wagner's operas with the curse of the gold, the tragic genius of Wotan, "all this world of blood-letting, killing the dragon, thirst for power, betrayal, sexuality, paganism and then the redemption and the bell-ringing on Good Friday—this was the environment that best corresponded to Hitler's angst and his need to triumph."[63]

Again, this is not a solid argument, rather an example of arm-chair psychology and guilt by association. But there is some truth to it, in the realm of trying to catch the complex phenomenon of Hitler's personality. Later on, apart from what this actually meant for Hitler and Nazism, Fest summarizes the tenor of Wagner's *oeuvre* rather well, at least some of it:

> Richard Wagner, like no one else, efficiently mobilized the magic of art against the ever-present tendency to realism, and translated into a myth this Zeitgeist had an overwhelming effect in his works:

---
[62] Fest p.60; translated by the author.
[63] Ibid p.67.

the pessimism regarding the future, the awareness of the increasing power of gold, the racial angst, the anti-materialistic trends, the fear of an age of plebeian freedom and levelling and the inkling of an impending doom.[64]

HISTRIONICS

From the perspective of "the world is a stage, the stage is a world" there are some similarities between Wagner and Hitler. Wagner condensed the world upon an opera stage and Hitler made Germany, indeed the whole of Europe and then some into his stage. I know I'm treading a fine line here, Wagner can't be blamed for the military parades etc. of the Nazis, but I have to quote the following from Fest. His book has some passages that are like essays, a word stemming from the French *essai*, attempt, and this is a fine attempt in catching the histrionic spirit of the Reich, a spirit that was partly Wagnerian:

> Just as Richard Wagner united the role of the revolutionary with that of friend of a king (...), so did the young Hitler dream of a career allowing his hatred of society to intermingle with his opportunism. Wagner nullified all apparent contradictions in his life by declaring art the goal of his life and proclaiming the artist as the highest authority, always prepared to lend a helping hand where "the statesman despairs, the politician lets his hands sink, the socialist torments himself with fruitless systems and isn't able to predict, only to indicate"; he proclaimed the total aestheticism of life under the leadership of art. Thus the state could be elevated to a work of art and the politics be rejuvenated by the spirit of art. In the theatricalization of public life in the Third Reich, the passion of the regime for grand stagings, in the drama of practical politics elements from this program shine forth with all due clarity.[65]

---

[64] Ibid p.112.
[65] Ibid p 60-61; translated by the author.

WAGNER DNA

How much or how little did Wagner and Wagner's music affect Hitler and the Third Reich? It isn't easy to say. Fest gives us some clues, a bit too far-reaching sometimes, but the mere character of this discussion—of delving into how art affects politics—probably must remain a bit vague, the discussion by necessity taking place in a land without clear borders. It's easier to discuss Hitler's economic and geopolitical ideas, for instance; these subjects are more clear-cut and easy to grip. Fest, although he seems to have an axe to grind, has sketched a general outline that seems feasible. He has taken us into the grey-area of where Wagner in some way influenced Hitler, and thus the Third Reich.

Additionally, it's interesting to see that Wagner's music didn't rule supreme in Nazi Germany. For example, Richard Evans [2005] is the source of the info that Wagner's popularity in the Reich declined in favour of Italian composers such as Verdi and Puccini. For example, in the 1938-39 season a Wagner opera was only one among fifteen productions, the most popular being Leoncavallo's *Pagliacci*. From another source I've heard that the Nazis from the beginning, 1933 and on, bombarded the German radio audience with Wagner, Bach, Beethoven and the likes. Then the regime realized that people need light entertainment also.

In Nazi Germany there was always the risk of a Wagner overdose. Wagner was a household word for the music of the day but among top Nazis not all shared Hitler's Wagner craze. Goebbels for one didn't, according to Spotts.[66]

In all fairness, Nazi Germany had some Wagner DNA in it. This you have to admit as a historian and a researcher. Now, as I said above, referring to Evans' 2005 study, there is no evidence that Hitler read Wagner's pamphlets. However, Wagner was indeed a polemicist while none of the other German 19th century composers were, not in the same degree. Wagner had opinions about this and that, some

---

[66] Bayreuth: A History of the Wagner Festival, 1999.

of them deemed controversial. Wagner was well footed in the grey-area of right-wing opinions, with ideas of race, German uniqueness and German supremacy. Wagner held many radical views and Hitler moved in the same areas of radicalism. Thus the association can be made.

"Wagner's influence on Nazi Germany" will always be a research field with vague borderlines. But "Wagner's influence on Hitler" is easier to sketch. For instance we have Rauschning's book, referred above, recording actual talks with Hitler. Hitler admiring Wagner as The Artist, the prophet of the German people: this might sound unpleasant to any music-lover content with going to the opera and being seduced by the wonders of Wagner's music, but the Wagner-Hitler connection remains a fact. I'm not saying that Wagner operas should be outlawed. But as a scholar and an informed every-man, being able to read and look around, I'd say that Wagner is and always will be controversial.

BEING PRO AND BEING ANTI

But wait; am I not being too facile in just saying that Wagner is controversial? What exactly is controversial? What opinions held by right-wingers aren't controversial these days?

There are some points that need to be clarified, as regards Wagner and as regards my own opinions. First I'd say, controversial or not, don't be "anti". Wagner held anti-Semitic views and I don't support these anti-Semitic views. Moreover, as an artist it's never fruitful to systematically envision what you *don't* like. Why, if I myself were to write a pamphlet on "the novel of the future", then I'd be an idiot if I structured the text according to what prose styles and narrative patterns I *don't* like, pointing at authors employing them. Or if I wrote on the spirituality of the future, then I wouldn't waste time on spiritual practices that are redundant. It's more fruitful to focus on what works and brings us forwards, stressing the positive and affirmative sides of the subject in question.

Be pro, not anti; that's the basic wisdom. But that doesn't take Wagner out of controversial territory.

I don't endorse the Wagner who was systematically against other peoples like the Jews. As for Jews in general, in the social realm he talked about assimilation but that too is a bit hostile. And having said that, it's also true that Wagner had controversial views of the affirmative kind. Like being a German nationalist. As you've seen in chapter 1 and elsewhere in this book I don't find nationalism per se controversial. To be what you are, to stand up for your people—a Japanese defending Japanese culture, a Chinese defending Chinese culture, an Iranian defending Iranian culture—what's wrong with that?

By this we approach the last step, the final frontier in controversy, 21st century style: not only to defend "your culture, your lifestyle", but your people too, your ethnicity—this is deemed forbidden for white people. In this respect, quoting from the UK newspaper Telegraph Wagner said this about ethnicity and nation (Telegraph for its part doesn't give the source for the quote):

> The *Volk* has always been the essence of all the individuals who constituted a commonality. In the beginning, it was the family and the races; then the races united through linguistic equality as a nation.[67]

The nations of the old world are defined by their ethnic specificity. "Nation" is derived from the Latin word "natio", to be born. A nation in this sense of the word is a group of people sharing a common ancestry. And nationalism is affirming your cultural, historical and ethnic heritage. There's nothing chauvinistic in this idea per se. A certain, limited amount of immigration could for example be fitted into the picture of a progressive nationalism.

So I'd say we have to reconsider the idea of nationalism always being controversial. I mean: a Japanese (Chinese, Iranian, Kurd etc.)

---

[67] http://www.telegraph.co.uk/culture/music/classicalmusic/8659814/Hitler-and-Wagner.html

defending the ethnic integrity of his people would be deemed OK, then why not a German?

Then some might say: "Germany" plus "nationalism" equals "Nazism". And I've been surveying the same ground in this chapter, saying that The Reich had some Wagnerian DNA in it. Now, I still mean that. But as for the nationalism of today I think it's time to lift the aura of taboo from it. We can't always arrange the debate about nationalism in accordance with those that have a mental blockage about it.

- - -

In being against the mass immigration of today's Europe you are labelled as this and that. But in what way, actually, is it controversial to stand up for the survival of your own people?

It would be rather interesting to get an answer to that question.

To conclude: in his writings Wagner was controversial in being systematically against Jewish music, and in sporting a hostile attitude towards Jews in general.

And maybe Wagner sometimes could be a bit chauvinist as regards the prowess of the German arms and as regards the specificity of the German people. But to stand up for your culture and people, as Wagner also did, this per se is not controversial. Be you German, Swedish, Iranian, Chinese or whatever.

In "Heldentum and Christentum" Wagner advocated the idea of a co-existence of peoples under the aegis of Christianity. Oh, controversial...! No, it's not. The definition of "Christianity" aside this is the essence of legitimacy and decency as I see it: a vision of peoples existing together in peace, led by a common idealistic framework, however not of the existing UN-NWO-globalist kind but of a more elevated, spiritual kind.

16. FRANCO-PRUSSIAN WAR

The war between France and Prussia was a watershed event in European history. By this victory Prussia-led Germany became a European great power, sporting nationalism as one of its dominant ideologies. Early on, long before nationalism became fashionable, Wagner had preached it explicitly and implicitly in his dramas. Implicitly: as writing an opera based on old German legends such as Nibelungenlied (The Ring). Explicitly: when Hans Sachs in *The Master-Singers* speaks about the need for a national German art.

Now, after 1871, nationalism in Germany became an officially endorsed idea. It hadn't been before, having been the exact opposite: in early 19th century Europe it was a revolutionary idea, a threat to the stability of nations. This we saw in 1848-49 when Wagner himself had been a revolutionary, having been chased away from Germany when the revolution had failed before the guns of Saxon and Prussian troops. Now, with the German Empire proclaimed in The Hall of Mirrors in Versailles in January 1871, the climate had changed rather dramatically. Wagner in being a nationalist became a German icon and his operas became the symbol of a resurgent German spirit.

Wagner for his part played along in this new climate. For instance, you could say that the nationalist Wagner had been in 1848 didn't dream about German unification being brought about by war. The young Wagner, I figure, was more of a populist idealist, dreaming of a German revival and unification being implemented more peacefully: "Einigkeit und Recht und Freiheit, für das deutsche Vaterland," as the German national anthem says, a song written by the liberal Hoffmann von Fellersleben in 1841. This more spiritual approach to German unification is more in sync with Wagner the artist, delving into politics most as a means to realize his own art.

KAISERMARSCH

As intimated, Wagner played along in the new, pro-Prussian climate. For example in the 1870's he asked Bismarck, the Prussian chancellor, for monetary contributions to his opera house in Bayreuth, completed in 1876. He eventually did get that. Wagner also wrote a *Kaisermarsch* to praise the symbol of the victory over France, kaiser Wilhelm I.

Thomas Mann has something to say about Wagner's nationalism at this time. It's in the essay "Richard Wagner's Suffering and Grandeur" from 1933 in *Wagner und unsere Zeit*. Wagner, according to Mann, saw the newly founded German *Reich* of 1871 as the right and true biotope for his cultural *oeuvre*. The reborn German state strengthened Wagner's belief in a German culture and a German art, that is, his own art and the possibilities of a serious opera. But even though Wagner got in line with the new regime, like composing the *Kaisermarsch*, Wagner wasn't accepted at once as a pillar of society. The role of the sacred national treasure he was to become at his death was still a bit distant. It was still hard to raise money for the Bayreuth opera house. Bismarck, the German chancellor and leading political figure, the symbol of executive power, according to Mann understood nothing of this upsurge of a German national art; Bismarck on the contrary saw Wagner as a mad romancer. But eventually the chancellor did subside Bayreuth along with many others.

So the connection between the German state, founded on war and symbolizing worldly power, and the Wagner *oeuvre*, based on reveries and romantic longing, isn't always that tight. But it's there; Wagner did affirm the German victory and Germany eventually took Wagner to his heart, celebrating itself with his *Festspieltheater*.

THE WAR

The Franco-Prussian war is sometimes called "the Franco-German war"; indeed, it ushered in the German Empire, to last 1871-1918. But the state proper warring against France in the 1870-71 conflict was called Prussia. This northern German state with Berlin as capital had been called Prussia since 1701. Before that it was called Brandenburg. In this chapter I'll use both *Germany* and *Prussia* for the German state who made war on France, although "Prussia" is the one correct name.

The war went on for about a year, between July 19, 1870, when France declared war against Prussia, and ended on May 10, 1871, when the treaty of Frankfurt was signed. Actual hostilities, including the siege of Paris, lasted for only about half a year. Operationally the war was even shorter since the German victory was virtually assured after the battle of Sedan, ending on September 2, 1870. Politically the war made possible the foundation of the German Kaiserreich. It also forced France's emperor Louis Napoleon to abdicate, igniting a process that made France into a republic. The regime change was made during the hostilities itself, in September 1870. And after some tribulations France from then on remained a republic, even to this day. But the constitution proper has been rewritten many times, last in 1958, ushering in the still existing Fifth Republic.

As for the origins of the Franco-Prussian war, there were some. I won't bother with them here. Suffice to say that France and Prussia were the two most powerful European nations by this time. Austria had been defeated by Prussia in a *blitzkrieg* in 1866 and was sitting idly by now as was Great Britain, not wishing to get involved on the continent. Bismarck's Germany was on the upsurge and a war against France would crown the wars of unification. Before the war against Austria Germany had defeated Denmark in another *blitzkrieg*, securing in the process some territory in the German-Danish borderland. As for Austria in 1866 no territory had been taken from it, it was just a war to decide which German state would be European hegemon. From France the border areas of Elsass and Lothringen (French: Alsace and Lorraine) would be annexed after the Franco-Prussian war.

Bismarck's war policy made the other German states rally around the Prussian flag, voluntarily or by necessity. For example, the ruler of the greatest German state after Prussia, Bavaria's king Ludwig, was not amused having to bow for Bismarck. But what could Ludwig do. He was a dreamer, content with building castles and staging Wagner operas. He had no interest in hands-on politics. He supported Prussia with troops and in exchange was given money so that he could build another fancy castle.

Bismarck, the chancellor of Prussia, used events (a certain candidature for the Spanish throne, the editing of a telegram from Prussia's king Wilhelm to Napoleon) to arouse anti-German feelings in France. Both countries were eager for war, public excitement was running high in both camps, but in the end it was France which declared war—as I said, on July 19, 1870. In the ensuing battles the French fought bravely but overall the French army was in need of reform, having rested on its laurels since the Napoleonic victories of 1799-1811. So the beginning of this war could be staged in tableaus of "French chaos at the mobilization versus the sure German concentration" and "French hopes of advancing towards Berlin being quelled by the parallel advance of three German corps". Indeed, the Germans soon crossed the border and all of the battles in the war were fought on French soil: Wissembourg, Montretout, St Privat, Sedan etc..

However, it was no picnic. The battles were bloody. It was like the American Civil War with old school infantry assaults being mowed down by long-range rifle fire. To this there were such novelties as German back-loaded artillery pieces and French machine guns (*mitrailleuse*).

The Germans won. The French capitulated. Germany could declare the inauguration of the German Empire in the Hall of Mirrors in Versailles on January 18, 1871, making the Prussian king Wilhelm into Kaiser Wilhelm I. Germany was made into an empire with Bavaria, Saxony, the Rhine states, Hannover, Lower Saxony and Thuringia as the most important parts, all led by Prussia as hegemonic power. Austria was not included. Only in 1938, with Hitler at the helm, would this other option, the "great German" solution be realized. The Germany that Bismarck now created, without Austria, was called the "small German" solution.

LUDWIG

As we saw in chapter 1 an attempt at unifying the German states came in 1848. By then, after the initial riots in diverse cities, an all-German parliament was gathered. But this congregation failed in unifying Germany. The parliament offered the German kaiser crown to Prussia's king Wilhelm but he turned it down. The wisdom gained by this by Prussia's prime minister Bismarck was that unification had to be done by force of arms, not by discussions in a parliament. Right or wrong, the unification soon got going with Prussia as the prime mover, fighting three wars.

As intimated, first Prussia brought Denmark to its knees, demanding some border provinces from the northern state as a token of the victory. Next Prussia defeated Austria in a lightning war. It was something of a political move, a serious display of arms intending to decide what land would exert hegemony over the German speaking lands, Prussia or Austria. Austria had hegemony since medieval times, now Prussia was the power on the rise.

Prussia won the war. Interestingly, the most powerful southern German state, Bavaria, had sided with Austria in this war of 1866. Now, in 1870, Ludwig had to bite the bullet and side with Prussia. He, along with the Bavarian elite, saw themselves as Germany's cultural consciousness and Prussia as northern barbarians. But necessity forced Ludwig to join the Prussian camp. Prussian nationalism aside, what should he have done? Sided with France? The Zeitgeist was against this kind of old-school cabinet policy. Nationalism was here to stay. For instance, at the same time Italy was unified as a national state. Now it was Germany's turn.

HERRENCHIEMSEE

Ludwig himself was payed handsomely by Bismarck to join the Prussian camp. A kind of bribe. It's said that Ludwig for this money built a copy of the French royal castle of Versailles, to be situated on an island in a Bavarian lake, the castle of Herrenchiemsee. Symbolically Ludwig by this achieved two victories: 1) his hall of mirrors was some additional meters longer than the original; take that, Louis XIV! 2) He got Bismarck to pay for an overall symbol of French cultural superiority; take that, Bismarck!

Ludwig's building of palaces was infamous. His mock-medieval castle on a high crag, Neuschwanstein, was said to have been partly inspired by a backdrop of a performance of Wagner's *The Master-Singers*. Ludwig's architect followed the general style of these supposed Nurembergian medieval fronts in envisioning the new castle, with their rows of windows with double round arches joined by a column. In all, with the steep roofs, the towers, the gatehouse and all the result is astonishing. This in itself is some kind of theatre architecture with the emphasis on effects, not on function. But it never pretended to be anything more. And on the pragmatic side this and other of Ludwig's building projects to this day are visted by hoards of tourists every year. I mean, the state of Bavaria in Ludwig's days was heavily indebted for this building craze but there is the possibility that it all has payed off financially by now.

A side-note on the finances: according to Wikipedia[68] regarding one of the building projects, Neuschwanstein, this may be said: "Ludwig paid for the palace out of his personal fortune and by means of extensive borrowing, rather than Bavarian public funds." The same source states that this structure was built as an homage to Richard Wagner. The palace is decorated with scenes from the Lohengrin legend, in the vein of Wagner's eponymous opera. Next to another of Ludwig's fancy castles, the classically styled Linderhof, there is an artificial grotto with a lake and a boat shaped like a cockleshell,

---

[68] Entry: Neuschwanstein Castle.

in which Ludwig himself sometimes sailed as Lohengrin. Like Lohengrin Ludwig was a kind of dream-knight, something right out of legend. In this he is the direct opposite of Bismarck. Bismarck was engaged in *realpolitik*, forging together Germany with blood and iron, a man with few or no cultural interests. Ludwig for his part had no talent for matters of state, instead spending his time with "crazy" projects like Neuschwanstein, Linderhof and Herrenchiemsee. And sponsoring Wagner and his operas.

Bismarck aside; Ludwig's castles were solidly built, they still stand and they still attract visitors. And Ludwig's sponsorship of Wagner was important in crowning that artistic project with success. Moreover, as a person Ludwig wasn't clinically mad, as he is sometimes labelled, he just had social phobia. This has got to be remembered when discussing this intriguing person.

17. WAGNER AND POPULAR CULTURE

The opera of today might be something of an elitist culture, a solidified and stylized art form locked in attitudes from the 19th century. Thus Wagner's operas might be seen as some kind of cultural relics, employing outdated attitudes and modes of expression. His opera as a whole didn't become "the artwork of the future" that he envisioned in his eponymous 1849 pamphlet. Nevertheless, in the cultural milieu of today some Wagnerian traits effortlessly live on. Implicitly we see this in modern film music. Explicitly we see it Wagner music used in film scores.

In this chapter I'll look into the popular character of Wagner's oeuvre. First, there's a discussion of Wagner's own ambitions to reach out to the people, his vision of a popular art, gathering high and low to his temple in Bayreuth. Then I look at how Wagner in the 20th century made his way into popular culture, in both cinema, rock music and literature.

POPULAR APPEAL

Sociologically speaking, Wagner's *oeuvre* seems to lack popular appeal. It's more or less an elite form of art. The opening of the Bayreuth *Festspiel* in 1876 for example was no folkfest. But it was intended as such, being a *Festspiel* for the people and not a court theatre. Mann (1963) for example tells about Wagner's plans for a theatre aimed at the people; from all over Germany and from all walks of life they would gather at the *Festspielhaus* and be taken away by the beauty of the artworks performed, an opera where the performers would sing and play for free.

But neither then nor now is Wagner opera a folk art. It can be described as an art form for the middle class and the well off. "Bayreuth was usurped by the bourgeoisie mob", Mann says. This can be said from the view of art sociology, even though at the same time you have to remember that Wagner's work is timeless and variegated, having something to tell everybody.

Mann: "Wagner's music is more national than folksy; true, it has many characters that *especially foreigners* perceive as German, but moreover it has an unmistakeable cosmopolitan flair."[69] Mann goes on to say that there are certain indigenous sounds in *The Master-Singers* and *Siegfried*, signatures triggering the listener's feeling into perceiving it as rustic and natural, but the fundamentals of Wagner's composing technique isn't especially folksy. See also *The Flying Dutchman*: there might be some Norweigian folk song-feeling to it, like in "Senta's Ballade", important as it is, but the style of "Chorus of the Norwegian Fishermen" is "European Opera", not folk art.

Nevertheless, Wagner is exerting his presence in contemporary popular art, discreetly but undeniably so.

HELICOPTERS ON THE COVER

Sometimes record companies compile "best of" collections with Wagner overtures and orchestral pieces. For example, today on the internet you can buy a compilation of Wagner orchestral pieces and overtures on CD, called *Twilight of the Gods: The Essential Wagner Collection*. The subtitle is: "Music of Terrifying Power and Transcending Beauty". It was originally issued in 1998 by Deutsche Grammophon, a venerable label for classic music. Here

---

[69] p.28.

we get standards such as "The Ride of the Valkyries", "Siegfried's Funeral March", "Siegfried's Rhine Journey", overtures to *The Flying Dutchman, Tannhäuser* and *The Master-Singers*, "Good Friday Music from Parsifal" and many more.

This all is very fine and proper. But the cover image might seem strange, sporting as it does American Bell UH-1 "Hueys" coming at you, the combat transport helicopter employed by US Army in Vietnam. However, the connection is apt; Francis Coppola's movie about the Vietnam War, *Apocalypse Now* (1979), in a scene uses "The Ride of the Valkyries" as a soundtrack. Technically this is not incidental, atmosphere-creating music but so called *source*, music actually played in the cinematic action itself, since the major in charge of the cavalry battalion in question has equipped his helicopters with loudspeakers that play the actual melody during assaults. This in order to scare the enemy.

When seeing the actual film I didn't quite like that scene, it gets a little over the top, something of an overstatement: "Look at the militarist Wagner's music being used in the most awful of all wars, how fitting...!" That said, now the connection is done—Vietnam War and "The Ride of the Valkyries"—so I have to admit that the CD in question having that film image of the helicopters, silhouetted against the sun, is very efficient. It's got edge, being a smart way of selling classical music to youngsters of today: "Wagner, terrifying power, awesome man..." I might cater to ulterior needs in saying this. But Wagner's music is rich and deep and it can withstand a lot, from stagings with modern props to CD covers with the war machines of the NWO.

EXCALIBUR

Wagner lived on, even in the 20th century, even beyond the opera stage. As for Wagner music used in soundtracks my best example is John Boorman's *Excalibur* (1981). True, this film also employs music from another classical composer, Carl Orff and his "O Fortunata" from *Carmina Burana*, since then a staple in circumstances like these. But the mainstay of the soundtrack is from Wagner. In scenes with Lancelot and Guinevere we hear the *Tristan* overture, and in sir Perceval's search for the Grail we hear, what else, the prelude to *Parsifal*.

Then there is the main theme, with parts of "Siegfried's Funeral March" from *Twilight of the Gods*. This music is heard at the beginning, with a text plate saying "The Dark Ages... The Land was divided and without a king", followed by rhapsodic scenes of fighting, of Merlin etc. The soundtrack to all this is Wagner and it's congenial. The same Wagner piece—the funeral march—is there at the end of the film, during the battle in which Arthur is killed by Mordred. Just before he dies Arthur tells Perceval to take Excalibur and throw it into the lake—the lake from which it once was given by the hand of the Lady of the Lake.

Eventually Perceval finds the lake and gets ready to throw the sword. At the same time, in anticipation, the hand of the Lady rises from the surface—and then we hear Wagner's "sword" leitmotif, flashing forth simultaneously as a light is reflected in the shiny blade during the throwing. It's almost better than a Wagner opera. Anyhow, Boorman succeeded in taking old music and having it fit like a glove to this scene, the sword leitmotif sounding out exactly when the hand of the Lady catches the hilt of the sword and then sinks with it, never to be seen again.

All this is very much in the spirit of Wagner. The music isn't ironically employed as in *Apocalypse Now*. This is the Wagnerian spirit, translated onto the screen, in a story that coheres. Then there is the employment of the leitmotif itself, Excalibur being a sword showcased with Wagner's sword theme: there is a chance of it getting too clever-clever, too contrived, but no, this just nails it, if I may say so. The use of classical music in *Excalibur* is on par with what Kubrick did in *2001*.

Boorman's *Excalibur*, by being produced in the pallid era of the early 1980's, with cold war, recession and unemployment, could have been a dour, anti-heroic, anti-romantic tale. But true artistry was about in writing the script, in producing and filming it so if you want to "get that Wagner feeling" on screen, in a non-operatic, modern, cinematographic way, go see *Excalibur*.

FILM MUSIC

Leitmotif, in case you didn't know already, is a musical phrase that symbolizes a person, a thing, a place or a feeling. Wagner didn't use the term itself but ever since the première of The Ring it's been widely used to characterize this Wagnerian effect. Musical phrases such as leitmotifs led an embryonic existence before Wagner but he made it into a modus operandi, slightly over-employing it, like in The Ring. However, after Wagner the leitmotif technique found its way into other musical areas than opera, preferably film music. To have a musical phrase repeating itself in the theme song (the, if you will, "overture") as well as here and there in the film score proper, became common practice after sound film came of age. For example the composer Bernard Herrmann (1911-1975), with film scores such as *Psycho* (1960) and *Vertigo* (1958), knew the Wagner way of making music. For instance, in the latter film there's echoes of "The Love-Death of Isolde" from *Tristan and Isolde*. Wikipedia[70] says that leitmotifs, in one sense or the other, have occurred since the advent of sound film:

> Erich Wolfgang Korngold's 1938 score for *The Adventures of Robin Hood*, for example, can be heard to attach particular themes and harmonies to individual characters: Robin, Will, Much, and Gisbourne are all accompanied by distinctive musical material. A more modern example is the *Star Wars* series, in which composer John Williams uses a large number of themes specifically associated with people and concepts (for example, a particular motif attaches to the presence of Darth Vader and another to the idea of the Force). In the film trilogy *Lord of the Rings* the dramatic orchestral score has hundreds of Leitmotifs recurring throughout.

---

[70] Entry: Leitmotif.

With the leitmotif technique in film music, I'd say the crux is not to overuse it. Overall there's a rule in putting music to film that goes: "don't Mickey Mouse it". You don't have to underline every motion or emotion with a musical phrase; conversely, in a cartoon the music *should* emphasize the motion in most respects. So, knowing that one or several leitmotifs, one or several recurring phrases, can be efficient in a film score the composer also should be aware of the risk of overemploying them. Wagner himself, too, can be prone to "Mickey Mousing it" in stacking leitmotifs upon each other, such as in the "Funeral March" of *Twilight of the Gods*.

Leitmotifs aside, the above mentioned John Williams has a very Wagnerian style in the use of the orchestra. True, there's a lot of Liszt in his "Star Wars Theme" too. And this was probably because the 1930's film serial Flash Gordon had employed Liszt's *Les Preludes* as a soundtrack. In any case, German 19th century symphonic music of the grand sort lends itself exquisitely to these kind of films, congenially called *space opera*.

As for popular cultural echoes of Wagner in rock music I'd like to mention the Slovenian group Laibach. In 2009 they created their *VolksWagner* suite with material from Wagner's operas. Generally it's hard to fuse classical music with rock but if there's a group that's able to tread this fine line I guess it's Laibach. In "rock meets classical music" the rock part tends to drown the classical part but Laibach has the courage to let the classical, string-and-horn-element lead. Basically it's symphonic music with the drum beat rather emphasized—not using synthetic drums, it's real percussion instruments, but underlining the music in a captivating, "catchy" and yet respectable fashion.

A NOVEL

Elsewhere in this book I take a look at a novel with a notable Wagner presence, *The Flame of Life* by d'Annunzio. Almost equally Wagner sub-themed is Lars Gustafsson's *The Tennis Players* from 1977. Now, d'Annunzio's novel was over 300 pages long and Gustafsson's is way shorter. And there might be other differences too, like plot wise and as concerns the narrative perspective. But the overall attitude and atmosphere of *The Tennis Players* reminds you of d'Annunzio's novel, being as it is energetic and optimistic, totally devoid of angst. Gustafsson's novel thus was a remarkable feat in itself, being issued in a time of economic recession, pessimism and defeatism. Every other serious novel of the Westworld of those days spelled doom and gloom, but not Gustafsson's. Even the first line of the book stands out, saying that *it was a happy time*. A remarkable opening for any novel of that time—for *any* novel of *any* time.

The first chapter tells about the narrator, being identical with Mr. Gustafsson, by the mid 70's living in Austin, Texas as a visiting university lecturer, tutoring in Swedish literature. He's inspired, he reads, writes and lectures, he plays tennis and jogs, and he goes down the lane in his ten-gear sports bike, whistling "Siegfried's Rhine Journey". Then he muses about this piece, doing it affirmatively and positively. That was rather unique for those days, the 70's, otherwise being something of a nadir for the Wagner reception. He was still performed but apart from opera-goers few took him seriously.

Wagner plays a role for the rest of the book too. A production of *The Rhine Gold* is in the offing, where the author among other things lets us know a bit about Wagner's radical sides, this being one way for 70's intellectuals to relate to Wagner. Along with the rest of the intrigue (where for example Strindberg's *Inferno* plays a role) *The Tennis Players* is recommendable as such, a learned yet readable novel, serious fiction in popular form.

18. ON BEING A GENIUS

The 30-year old Wagner was something of a populist revolutionary, envisioning a Germany run by, for and with the people. Down with the rule of reactionary monarchs, down with official religion; let the free spirit of German *Volkstum* come to the fore. Later on Wagner kept some of his populist ideals, like wishing that the Bayreuth Festspiel would be a festival for the people. It turned out not to be, becoming instead a bourgeois festivity. And by this time—the 1870's —Wagner had sided with the establishment, not any longer sporting ideals of social progress and humanistic development. In his Wagner bio[71] Hans Mayer intimates that, like Schopenhauer, the mature Wagner didn't think that progress was possible in the domain of social issues. No, the only progress is that of the genius...! He should be given a free reign in order to bring humanity onward to greener pastures, if there are any.

Wagner was breaking something of a taboo here, even more so in the light of 20th and 21st century thought. The great spirits, those giving the world new impulses, act on their own accord despite all hardships, despite the current trends and predilections of the people. The genius is the informal leader of the people. Nothing will be done without great men like Bach, Beethoven, Goethe, Shakespeare—and Wagner. Wagner mused over such ideas. And he was right in doing it. The genius makes his own laws. Being his own most rigorous teacher he walks the road that intuition points out to him, leading him and

---

[71] p.164.

eventually his people, indeed all people, to new domains, new vistas, new sounds.

HANS SACHS

At the end of *The Master-Singers* the main character, Hans Sachs, sings an aria. The nationalist ideas of this are often quoted, I even do it myself, see chapter 9. There I also quote Sachs praising the genius and the artist: *Verachtet nicht die Meister, ehrt ihre Kunst!* Art accomplishes more than politics and war. The artist is the true aristocrat, a figure leading the people forwards with his visions.

This is central for understanding Wagner. We should honour the great artists, solitary minds performing esoteric feats. Personally I'd say that Wagner represents the genial artist creating while in trance. The role of the true artist is transcendental, it's spiritual, the artist being a sort of shaman that gathers unique visions while roaming the astral world. While out on his quests this shaman sees the essence of things, catching a glimpse of the Platonic idea. And back in his studio the artist gives this vision shape, adding something of his own nature to it. Plotinos knew this, Goethe and Schelling knew this, even Schopenhauer, d'Annunzio and Ernst Jünger knew this. This is the art theory of *philosophia perennis*.

THE CULT

At the end of his life Wagner became the centre of a cult. Bayreuth was the temple, the operas the liturgy and he himself the high priest, insisting on being called "master". This might seem a bit over the top but in essence, this is what any artist worthy of his name wants: to be the centre of a cult. It might seem unhealthy and it might lead to sclerosis and ritual, but if you have a tinge of humour in it such a cult is to be encouraged. However, I have the inkling that there was no element of humour or self-irony in the Wagner cult. His insisting on being called "master" is an indication of that. He took it a bit too far.

TO BE AN ARTIST

"On Being a Genius" is the headline of this chapter. It could also have been, "to be an artist". This we tend to forget, that Wagner was an artist first and foremost. Wagner himself is partly to blame: with his activities as polemicist and pamphleteer, and as the composer of "Kaisermarsch" and the poem "To the German Army Before Paris", he comes forth as the politically inclined person, a role tending to obscure his role as an artist, a man first of all focused on creating works of art.

After his death Wagner became a monument, the stern, solid, image of a man who could do no wrong, a fierce man having walked his lonely road from obscurity to stardom. The heroism of his life path is there but it isn't all of the truth. Wagner was a musician bent on composing operas, and with this goal he arranged his life. The political element can't be denied, see for example his partaking in the 1848-49 revolution, but as Mayer has indicated Wagner tended to see the revolution as *his* revolution: what could the revolution give him, Wagner, concerning his ideas for a new operatic art?

Wagner was an artist. The artist's lifestyle isn't always so heroic. Baudelaire for one called the artist's condition, "systematically regained childishness". Wagner wasn't exactly childish but he had traits of the bohème, the careless spender, all in order to install a creative atmosphere—an atmosphere where he could write his operas. Judging from his memoirs an ideal day spent by Wagner would begin by doing some composing, then taking a walk, then maybe go to the theatre, read novels etc. There's nothing heroic or monumental in that per se. This is the image of his daily life we get glimpses from in *Mein Leben*. At the same time Wagner in this book construed himself into the ever sure, ever determined hero who never faltered, but between the lines we read of a man who lived in his dreams and thoughts, an impractical man of visions and ideas that sometimes was in harmony with the Zeitgeist, sometimes against it.

THE MUSES

In his memoir Wagner becomes the Monument. Already while he lived he had these self-promoting, ego-boosting traits, such as I mentioned above: of making his artwork into a cult and insisting on calling himself "master". But again, he was no saint so this might be forgiven him. He was true to his artistic visions; he didn't compromise, not alarmingly much.

Wagner wasn't a saint. Nor was he altogether a political person, a German Nationalist Type 1A, although traits of that emerged late in his life. In fact, earlier he had said to Liszt, "a political person is despicable".[72] Here we find a clue to a side of Wagner that tends to be neglected. Wagner was a serious artist, a man steeped in classical German culture (Goethe Schiller, Bach, Beethoven) but this doesn't make him into an enemy of Freedom, Naturalness and Spontaneity, as some people wary of all things German might think. Wagner was a man with gravitas and pathos, comedy didn't come natural to him (although *The Master-Singers* has a lightness of touch that is admirable), but the core of all his doings is the artistry, the musical feeling, *der Geist der Musik* as Nietzsche would say. "Music" comes from the Greek word *muse*, a goddess inspiring man to works of literature, science and art. And Wagner, in combining several art forms in his *Gesamtkunstwerk*, was truly loved by the muses.

According to the more ambitious interpretation there were nine muses. Two of them he didn't live under: Urania, the muse of astronomy and Clio, the muse of history. But Wagner—I'd say—stood under the auspices of the rest of them, namely: Calliope (epic poetry; Wagner told stories), Euterpe (song; Wagner composed music), Erato (lyric poetry; at their best Wagner's libretti are singable poetry),

---

[72] Fest 1974, p.429.

Melpomene (tragedy; the mainstay of Wagner's dramas are essentially tragedies), Polyhymnia (hymns; *The Master-Singers* has a hymn to German culture at the end, *Parsifal* praises the spiritual power of the Grail, love duets in *Tristan* etc. are hymns to love). Finally we have Terpsicore, the muse of dance and Thalia, the muse of comedy, and both these are represented in *The Master-Singers*, a comedy sporting a ballet: *Tanz der Lehrlinge*.

To sum it up, Wagner stood under the influence of seven muses. This, to me, is the essence of what "Wagner" means. This is what he represents, the *sine qua non* of his life and work: art and artistry, the artistic way of life, the genius fashioning his life according to the spirit of music.

19. SCENOGRAPHY

I once commented something on the internet about the ugliness of modern Wagner productions. A friend then tipped me of a Facebook site called "Against Modern Opera Productions". I looked it up and truly got to see some awful modern opera scenography. This site was about opera in general, the aesthetic phenomenon in question being endemic to contemporary opera. Ugliness is all-pervading.

As for Wagner productions the site also had some examples of this. There were new, horrid ones and there were older, classy ones. Indeed, Wagner takes out both the best and the worst of scenographers. But it isn't so easy such as, "in the past everything was good, now everything is bad".

I've thought about this phenomenon for some time. In fact, ever since I saw a certain picture in a schoolbook, back in the Swedish 1980's: on the one hand there was a picture of a naturalistic scenery from a 19th century production of *Siegfried*, with the hero walking through a lush forest, on the other a 1950's Bayreuth production of *Tristan and Isolde*, with the pair lying prostrate on a circular, totally clean stage, very minimalistic.

Thus, to begin with, we have traditional stagings from, say, before 1945, more or less following the stage directions in Wagner's libretti. Then we have the 1950's minimalism of Wieland Wagner's productions. Then we have the post-modern style with "putting everything on stage". Also, we have a moderate traditionalist style still being used, even today, a style that flies under the radar of critics. For example, the CD *Wagner—Opera Choruses* (2003), issued by the Royal Swedish Opera, on the cover depicts a 21st century Swedish staging of Wagner (I have a hard time finding out from which opera though, maybe it's *Lohengrin* or *Rienzi*) with the cast clad in medieval robes and standing among props of ancient buildings. So the trait of dressing up Wagner in traditional garb hasn't died out completely. It's still there as a possibility, even in the 21st century.

And as intimated, I won't close the door on modern/postmodern scenography altogether. The crux for any Wagner scenographer, to me, is this: make it work, make your scenery harmonize with the spirit of Wagner's intention. The general advice would be: go to the libretto, read it, listen to the music, and then ask yourself: is the best stage for this a multi-story car park, a power plant and a vacant lot on the outskirts of town? If the answer is yes, then go for it. This modern approach can engender alluring and captivating scenery too.

PARSIFAL ON THE MOON

Then again, you mustn't be locked in a style. But today the modern/postmodern style seems to be the *default mode* of scenographers. As for high-profile Wagner productions, especially in Europe (Bayreuth, La Scala), it would seem that the producers are locked in mannerisms, bordering on the ugly. The syndrome might be described as this: the common artist-cum-intellectual of the European kind is imbued with ideas of how dangerous it is to affirm the traditional side of things, especially when it comes to Wagner. Therefore scenery Type 1A tends to be "denigration of Wagner's oeuvre by putting a hot dog stand on stage".

That's how it tends to be in Europe. In the USA on the other hand the producers seem to be a bit more free from this obsession. True, The Metropolitan in New York weren't traditional in staging Parsifal in 2013 with a landscape reminiscent of the moon, the characters going about bare-foot. That said the scenography was original and true to Wagner's spirit in almost every sense, in fact, overall taking his work to another level. The 1880's costumes to Parsifal were congenial (medieval castle, medieval frocks) but the Met here showed us that you can make it new and make it work. This the Met also did in its 2010 production of The Ring: traditional, medieval-style costumes in a high-tech scenery that followed Wagner's intentions congenially, taking the work into the 21st century while at the same time keeping the archaic spirit of it alive. The Valkyries for example wore armour and sported long hair, just as I personally think they should do. The costumes were all early medieval in character, all fantasy-styled: archaic. Not a three-piece suit, ice hockey helmet or welder's goggles as far as the eye could see. But all the rest—the props and the scenography, the Valkyries' horses, the Rhine etc. clearly employed high-tech in an indescribable, creative fashion.

Everything isn't bad today. Kudos to The Met I say.

COSTUME DESIGN

The common scenography style of today is "make it new, make it modern". But to give more fuel to it, more life, I think a spate of archaism is needed; synonyms to "archaism" might be "ancientness, hoariness, antiqueness, elderliness". Guillaume Faye springs to mind here. Recently he said: "[F]uturism must be *tempered* with archaism; or to use a bold expression, we might say that *archaism must cleanse futurism*."[73]

It was in *Archeofuturism* (2010) that Faye developed his idea of balancing futurist and modernist approaches with ancient, archaic traits – in one word, archeofuturism. And there is one Wagner opera production that to me seems to have fused futurism with archaism into a durable alloy: The Ring on Covent Garden in London 1976, directed by Götz Friedrich and with Josef Svoboda as scenographer.

Friedrich wanted to let the succession of the four operas of the cycle make a virtual journey through time, through successive epochs,

---

[73] Faye 2010, s 72.

letting *The Rhine Gold* represent primeval times and *Twilight of the Gods* the future. In line with this the costume designer, Ingrid Rosell, settled for a "credible anachronism which by the shape, colour and style could give associations to both present and saga times. I wanted to create a fabric of modern and old shapes so intricately weaved together that it could be experienced as a credible whole, easy to feel familiar with and at the same time incredible and fantastic as The Ring itself."[74]

By this we got a production mixing styles, however, with the overall look having a taste of fantasy and saga, sporting wing helmets, flowing cloaks and fancy weapons with archaic feeling. Along with this we had modern elements like the goggles of Alberich and Fafner and Fasolt in football helmets. As intimated the director, Friedrich, wanted the past to play along with contemporary times and the future so these modern elements, today the staple ware of Wagner costumes, seem to have had their première under Rosell's auspices. Therefore I bow to her costume making; she was original, she let the forms flow. Artistic freedom.

At the same time Rosell was no dyed-in-the-wool Wagner lover, on the contrary, she was critical of what she calls Wagner's fascist traits. But the resulting costumes don't show the sign of her having an axe to grind. So along with Svoboda's ingenious scenography this production became a functioning whole. Svoboda's stage solutions were rather heavy on square shapes, they had some emphasis on contemporariness and futurism. However, alluding to Faye you might say that the *archaism* of Rosell's costumes somewhat cleansed Svoboda's *futurism*.

UPDATING TRADITIONALISM

The Covent Garden production fused archaism with futurism. And this now is common practice among Wagner scenographers. Along with having the operas dressed in contemporary clothes—three piece suits, overalls and everything, maybe barring jeans—the total blending of all styles tends to be the standard way to go. But it isn't

---

[74] Rosell p.10; translated by the author.

the only way to go. There is also the possibility of staging, say, The Ring in thorough fantasy style. A Ring for the Tolkien generation, if you will, for people like me steeped in the venerable Oxford author's trilogy as well as works by Le Guin, Moorcock and Lord Dunsany, novels of fairy lands that you still can relate to.

I mentioned The Ring on The Metropolitan in 2010 above. This production had 1) traditional costumes 2) scenography affirming square shapes, "a machine feeling". And as traditional costumes in these cases often is a neglected possibility this was a gladdening surprise. As for the modern looking scenography, also employed by Svoboda in 1976, I say: Okay. Wagner's stage directions need ingenuity to work so modern stage technology should as a principle be affirmed. That said, overall modern Wagner scenography seems to be locked in mannerisms. I'd say, there is more to gather in sceneries that have an element of fantasy, wonder and glory in them. I say this in the hope of having modern Wagner scenographers widening their aesthetic vision; make a more traditional approach and awe at the possibilities of showing woodland, mountains and boundless nature, of magic and fairytale visions. Something of this needs to be translated into modern productions.

It's once again time for a traditionally designed Ring with backdrops of woodland and castles *and* singers in medieval clothing. That was how the operas were envisioned at the beginning. A symbolic event occurred when the traditional, 1800's costumes and props until then used in Bayreuth, were plundered by American soldiers during the offensive into Germany in 1945.

The old costume supplies were scattered. Brünhilde with braids, helmet and cuirass became history. It was perhaps just as well. And after that we got the minimalist approach of 1950's Bayreuth, we got experimental scenography. And then the post-modernist style became a manner. Today producers seem to be able to do anything, except for using thorough archaic aesthetics. Today's producers are obsessed with post-modernity.

There's a time for everything. And now, not as an imperative style, not as a binding commission to "northernness", "archaism" or whatever, but as a possibility, I think it's time for going all the way with the fantasy-cum-medieval style. Once again it's time for a traditionally costumed ring, a ring for the role-play, World of Warcraft and fantasy literature generation. A ring with woodland and mountains, a Ring with tunics, breeches, wing helmets and chemises, frocks and burnooses. As long as they avoid a Brünhilde in braids it will all be fine. And The Met in 2010 did just that: no braids on Brünhilde, Deborah Voigt just letting her auburn tresses flow. Nice and archaic and not feeling like a 19th century production.

I mean, to "go archaic" isn't about re-creating the Bayreuth style of 1876. It's about a carefully updated traditionalism. For instance, *The Lord of the Rings* movies gave the early medieval atmosphere a fresh look. Contemporary opera producers should be able to do something similar for The Ring–like the Metropolitan just did, but also adding archaic scenography with woodland, cliffs and old-school castle interiors.

20. ON WAGNER'S MUSIC

Wagner wrote music for the unmusical. This is according to Theodor Adorno (1964).

The statement is true in a way. Take the case of myself. Now I wouldn't say that I'm unmusical. For instance, I can sing rather well. But I can't read notes and I wasn't drawn into Wagner's world on purely musical grounds. No, it began by reading about his Ring epic. And Wagner in his essays on aesthetics expressly stated that in the opera the lyrics comes first, the music second. He toned down this statement later in life. The Ring has rather many free-standing orchestral pieces, a trait said to mirror Wagner's freshly roused belief in the power of music per se. Schopenhauer was the impulse-giver of this.

However, in Wagner's work as a whole, in his creative process writing operas the drafting of the libretto came first, then the music was composed. And in *Music of the Future* (*Zukunftsmusik,* 1860) he for example attacks the idea of program music, a trend in 19th century music trying to musically render an extra-musical narrative. True, the trait was there even earlier but it blossomed in the 1800's with such works as Beethoven's *Pastoral Symphony* (Symphony No. 6), Berlioz' *Symphonie fantastique* and Mussorgsky's *Pictures at an Exhibition*. The latter was issued in 1874, well after Wagner wrote in 1860, but Beethoven's and Berlioz' program pieces were out by then. And Wagner's friend Liszt was well into this genre.

In fact, Liszt made several condensed symphonies called *symphonic poems*, all led by an extra-musical narrative or idea. And his mainstay in this respect, the first 12 symphonic poems, were composed in the decade 1848-58. Wagner however wasn't ecstatic about them, shown in the essay "On Franz Liszt's Symphonic Poems" (1857). And in his pamphlet on the music of the future Wagner says, "Not a Programme can speak the meaning of the Symphony; no, nothing but a stage-performance of the Dramatic Action itself."[75] The "endless melody", discreetly leading the listener along in a stage drama, is The Music of the Future, Wagner means.

Liszt[76] opposed Wagner in this respect. Liszt wanted to fuse poetry and music in his symphonic poems, being purely musical creations but with an underlying narrative or idea. And I must say, the Liszt approach is overall concise and elegant. In listening to his *Tongedichte*, like *Les préludes, Mazeppa* and *Tasso,* the program triggers the inner eye to envision the story in question—but discreetly, only by means of the title and the music itself. You don't need a stage, props, singers and a libretto to follow.

Opera will live on, in one or the other form—like musicals —but the Wagner approach to music per se, stressing the text and advocating a discreet endless melody, seems to lead nowhere. True, Wagner operas are still performed en masse. But musically his work often tends to live on in fragments. The mainstay of Wagner music on CD is a de-constructed Wagner. Random Wagner CD is a greatest hits compilation, a collection of overtures and orchestral pieces. The vocal element sometimes seems to be redundant. For instance, I've seen examples of recordings like "The Rhine Gold Without Words".

Where does this take me? It takes me to the land of program music. And this music, even in the venerable form Liszt gave it, still is a kind of "music for the unmusical". It's music that gives people like me, with a need for images and sceneries, an entry to the land of music. Of course I can also appreciate classical works that only says

---

[75] Quoted after Wikipedia, entry: Music of the Future.
[76] Ibid.

"Opus X in Y minor", but it gets a lot more fun to have a program underlining the music. The music that only is music, absolute music, may be the ideal form of music, "expressions of the first emanations of the World Spirit" as Schopenhauer would have it. But personally I have easier to relate to program music.

The subject of this book, Wagner, as we've seen was against the idea of program music. But—as intimated—aside from his life on today's opera scenes, a vital existence by all standards, the Wagner we usually meet on recordings is something of a de-constructed, program music Wagner. His four-five hour operas don't fit into the manageable form of one CD. Mostly it takes three or four. But a Best of Wagner compilation beautifully fits into one CD. As does a sample of Lizst's *Tongedichte*, the pieces being about 15-20 minutes long. As such this form, program music, eased the pressure on classical composers to write symphonies. After Beethoven the art of the symphony more or less peaked, it was a bit hard to say anything new with this form. The symphonic poem gave the answer: a piece with a symphonic approach but allowing the composer to condense the whole into half the length of a real symphony.

21. WAGNER AND LITERATURE

One of the venerable sources for this book has been Hans Mayer's Wagner biography from 1959. Another has been Thomas Mann's Wagner book from 1963, *Wagner und unsere Zeit*. Hereby some ideas and thoughts from these books concerning the literary character of Wagner's work.

MUSICAL NOVELS

Wagner's opera was carried by a literary feeling, being a kind of novelistic art like Flaubert's. Wagner's dramas are musical novels, Mayer says. Mann (1963) is touching on the same trait when he compares Wagner's role to another French novelist, Émile Zola (1840-1902). Wagner wrote his four-part Ring cycle, Zola his cycle of novels about the Rougon-Macquart.

Mann for his part appreciated Wagner as an epic narrator. The leitmotifs, the wordy cross-references, the symbolic formula—this inspired Mann the epic novelist. And Wagner probably is alone among composers in being such a literary gifted artist. This Wagner acknowledged himself. His oddity of starting out as a dramatist, of first writing a play (*Leubald*) before he began to compose, is one testimony of this.

As a young student Wagner was influenced by Shakespeare, Mayer says. Wagner, starting to write dramas before he could compose music, eventually became a master of both drama and composition, truly unique in the history of art. He wrote his own libretti, the text came first, then the music was laid out in accordance to the plot, even according to the verse. Music was secondary to literature; music was the woman who was impregnated by literature, the man, Wagner meant. This in contrast to Mozart who, concerning operas, said that "the text shall be the obedient daughter of the music". However, aren't these just different approaches to the creative process, mirroring the respective artist, not artistic laws...?

EXPLAINING THE PLOT

Wagner's operas have the nature of musical novels, as intimated above. The operas aren't exactly born out of the spirit of music but out of an urge to explain something. Lundewall says that Wagner made long operas because he didn't want to get misunderstood. Wagner took his time explaining the plot. For this the endless melody and the ever ongoing speech-song might be needed.

Of course, you can't reduce Wagner into a school-master tutoring the audience with plots supported by music. But his approach to opera is somewhat original. And maybe redundant. The art of opera more or less peaked with Wagner.

Throughout this book I've discussed the plots of Wagner's opera rather thoroughly. For instance I've noticed that all of his operas have three acts. Maybe all operas have, I don't know. The three-act pattern however is a tried way of telling stories: the beginning, the middle and the end. This shouldn't be taken as the only way of structuring a story. But for the beginner it's a starting point.

TOLKIEN

Mann and Mayer likened Wagner's art to epic novels. Mann for his part mentioned Zola's Rougon-Macquart cycle. This one had about 20 novels in it. Okay. But you could also compare Wagner to Tolkien, who like Wagner wrote a trilogy; Wagner only thought of *The Rhine Gold* as a foreplay, thus The Ring can be seen as a trilogy. I've already mentioned Tolkien in the chapter about The Ring. Here it could be added: in essence Wagner and Tolkien are on par as traditionally oriented story-tellers.

Personally I've always enjoyed The Ring as a story. As I said in the introduction my first encounter with Wagner was in the form of an illustrated classic. This concise summary still had all the elements in it, the whole of it sporting epic quality. And in skipping to mention that it all ends with Wotan meeting his end in a burning Valhalla, this in turn spelling the end of the world with everything going up in *Ragnarök* flames, this illustrated comic book version of the story became more manageable, more relatable. It ended with Hagen sinking into the Rhine and the Rhine Maidens reclaiming their gold. The makers of this series had truncated the ending but it made perfect sense anyhow. Wotan still figured in it, all his crucial scenes were there, but the end was shortened and the whole of it thus became a human drama more than a divine drama. That's how it should be done, as intimated in the chapter about The Ring: don't cast gods in the central roles, only let them appear briefly while human beings take up centre stage.

That said, Wagner in fusing The Poetic Edda, Snorre's Edda, Volsunga Saga and Nibelungenlied has constructed a story of some value. His Ring is now part of the ancient Nordic heritage. C. S. Lewis called the Wagner-Tolkien etc.. genre *Northernness*, sporting that archaic, early medieval, rustic feeling. And as such both Tolkien and Wagner engendered many secondary artistic impressions, renderings in pictorial form, in the case of Wagner for example represented by Arthur Rackham. But there are many others. And these can serve you as inspirations to read the basic documents (the Edda etc.) as well as lead you into Wagner's work as a whole.

MIME ARTIST

Wagner had a penchant for absorbing things. I've touched on this before. First he writes operas in the grand, European style; then he gets enmeshed in mythology and writes about medieval heroes, then he's said to have become "a Schopenhauerian", then he's into Northernness and an embryonic Asatru, then it's Christianity. And all the time the result is spotless but a wee bit lifeless.

Sometimes I'm asking myself: who is this Wagner? What's behind the facade? Of course we have pervading themes like swans, fatherless young men and love conquers all. But, I mean, why did he always work on ready-made, already existing stories? A quote from Jeanson can clarify the matter. Jeanson here focuses on the musical side of it but this might also give some clues as to Wagner as an epic narrator:

> [The artist type Wagner represented] was apprehended by Nietzsche when he in Wagner saw a genius actor, a master of interpretation. A modern German critic, Paul Bekker, went a step further in this direction when characterising the artist type embodied by Wagner as a mask or a mime. (...) [Wagner wasn't a primarily creative genius like Bach, Mozart or Beethoven.] Wagner, as it were, assimilates the power he needs in order to fashion something artistically; he has the mime's ability to mimic, to reshape expressive powers according to his artistic intention and in the most variegated way. (...) Listening to Wagner's music you get the ineluctable impression that it stems not from a purely musical source but rather being a sort of "backdrop art", permeated by a highly subjective intensity.[77]

Wagner absorbs things, he embodies existing story structures as if they were his own creations. He assimilates what he needs in order to express himself, reshaping traditional stories into narratives that sometimes tells us something, sometimes maybe not.

In this book I've stressed Wagner the writer, how good he was at outlining prose drafts, good at writing versified stories (librettos), but at the same time it gets a little mechanical. Now, I will always like *Parsifal*, it still is stage magic, but like most other Wagner operas it

---

[77] Jeanson p.67-68; translated by the author.

has the character of "a good adaptation", I figure. Sometimes you don't have to be original, true that, but my own approach to writing has always, in some manner, been: make it new. If I love, say, medieval legends, magic and all, then a fantasy setting in a parallel world might be more feasible, like Tolkien showed us. Tolkien like Wagner was steeped in tradition but he didn't stage a story about early medieval Europe, he created a world of his own.

You might say that Tolkien, as traditional as he may have been, in his overall approach heeded the modernist call of "making it new". And in the same vein, in looking at Wagner with all his adaptations, his keeping the narratives confined within their given limits; this makes Wagner a little less than great. Maybe I've obsessed with "making it new". But Wagner in this adaptive craze, in this approach devoid of starting from a clean slate, makes him seem a bit dated. Or, modern or not, a bit unoriginal. A mime artist being absorbed in this and that, but where's the core?

THE POET

As for Wagner the poet I've quoted a lot of his librettoes in this book. True, he wrote singable poetry but is Wagner's poetry viable as such, on its own merits? Or is it just "traditional 19th century poetry, standard fare"? I don't know. But single lines and titles have their simple poetic power, this I have to admit. I can't altogether discard a creator of lines like "Abendlich strahlt der Sonne Auge", "Dich, teure Halle, grüss' ich" and "Wahn! Wahn! Überall Wahn!"

51%

Towards Wagner as a poet, a narrator (and musician) I'm, let's say, 51% positive. I won't compare him to other composers or writers. Wagner *is*, period. He has fascinated me for 30 years and hopefully there's still some magic left in his work for me.

With Wagner the writer it may be as with Wagner the musician. As I said about the *Rienzi* overture in chapter 3 this piece both shows us what's good with Wagner and what's bad: captivating and alluring and at the same time a bit contrived and fashioned. You'll have to live with this, even when it comes to Wagner the story-teller: he couldn't create a totally original narrative, he had to rely on some existing legend or story. I mean, "Wagner characters" like Wotan, Brünhilde, Siegfried and Parsifal have made a lasting impression on me and then I'll have to live with the fact that he worked on existing narratives and characters, not being totally able to "make it new".

22. MISCELLANEOUS

n this chapter I collect reflections and facts that don't seem to fit in anywhere else. I'll be looking at things such as Wagner's seriousness, Bayreuth and Swedish Wagner productions

- - -

Wagner built his own opera house in Bayreuth, Bavaria. I have touched on it before in this book. In chapter 15, for example, I mentioned the controversial aspects of Bayreuth's history, like Hitler's visit to the festival and Villa Wahnfried. Here I'll mention other facts of this Wagner watering place.

The Bayreuth opera house opened its doors in 1876. From then there's been a music festival—*Bayreuther Festspiele*—almost annually at this venue. 1944 saw the last festival for a while. Then, in 1951, the shows got going again, uninterrupted until this day.

The opera house proper had its novelties. Like no gallery, all the seats being placed on the amphitheatre's rising floor, and the concealing of the orchestra from the spectator's view.

- - -

In 1851 Wagner published the polemical work *Opera and Drama* (*Opera und Drama*). According to Mayer Wagner in this essay envisioned *a future art, liberated by revolutionary re-disposition*. For instance, the concept of "opera" (Ger. Opfer) would have to go, leaving room for "the music drama". From other sources I gather that Wagner later in his life abandoned this terminology; then it was okay to call his works "operas" again.

- - -

In chapter 17 I looked into Wagner's role in the popular perception. Seen from his own standpoint Wagner tried to reach out to all and sundry, wishing the *Bayreuther Festspiel* to become a beacon for the whole German nation, gathering both high and low to be united in national spree. This didn't happen, the Wagner oeuvre got co-opted by the middle class as I mentioned. And seen from the other aspect, that of seriousness and pathos instead of folksiness and popular appeal, Wagner did indeed have a serious approach. This would rather be his *sine qua non*, if anyone now thinks that populism is the gold standard of art.

Seriousness: Mayer says that Wagner worshipped the classic German art, such as Goethe, Schiller, Beethoven and Weber. This elevated artistic approach could explain why Wagner wasn't well received in Paris at first. As intimated the French audience wanted gaieté and a good show, not pretentious, ponderous music dramas.

Even as a young artist Wagner had *pathos*. I've said that in chapter 1. Goethe, Schiller, Shakespeare, Bach and Beethoven: this was the ideal, this was the atmosphere in which he lived. But the theatre and opera of his day wasn't normally into this kind of *gravitas*. Either lowly populist art or Grand Opera with empty pomp and circumstance (Meyberbeer) was what the producers wanted.

Wagner operas carry a certain dignity about them. This dignity is more or less absent in French and Italian opera. Okay, Verdi has his moments. Bayreuth, the opera as a temple, was an idea growing out of the German *Geist*. The same, Mann intimates, was the case in ancient Greek drama. The tragedies of Aischylos had pathos and gravitas. With Bayreuth something of this was reborn—not perfect in all details, but sufficiently to be noteworthy. Wagner's hieratic genius made Bayreuth into a latter-day mystery place, as such elevated above other theatres.

Mann makes this point: Goethe in his day had similar ambitions about theatre. Goethe in staging dramas in Weimar wanted them to be serious, stressing the sacrality of performing tragedies. But a certain producer there at Weimar didn't get it, instead being bent on having silliness at the forefront, like having a trained poodle as a stage hero.

- - -

In Portuguese The Ring is called *Anel dos Nibelungos*. As a poet I like the sound of that combination.

- - -

Wagner in a letter to Minna in 1858, their marriage all but crashed, says he's ready not for the sanatorium but for the madhouse. My reflection: Richard Wagner was no mere salon dweller, enjoying life as if on a holiday. He was there, in the harsh psychological reality of madness and bliss and everything in between. He never got clinically mad but as intimated in chapter 5 his was a restless spirit, the opera *Tannhäuser* being "a reflection of Wagner's own, hysterically unbalanced nature, oscillating between eros and Ethos, Wagner himself describing his nature as "nie und nirgends etwas nur ein wenig, sondern alles voll und ganz" ("Never and nowhere just a little, but everything to the fullest").[78]

- - -

I'm a Swede. And as for the performance history of Wagner in Sweden there's a lot to be said. For example, Stockholm's royal opera has produced Wagner since playing the Tannhäuser overture in a

---

[78] Jeanson p.74; translated by the author.

concerto in February, 1856. This according to Stefan Johansson in the liner notes to the CD "Wagner Opera Choruses" (2004). At first the staging of the operas *Rienzi* and *The Flying Dutchman* (the latter in 1872) weren't popular, Johansson goes on to say, but with the 1874 performance of *Lohengrin* Wagner got his Swedish breakthrough.

At the end of the 19th century a new opera house was built, the one still standing in Stockholm City close to the Royal Castle and the Riksdagshuset. And Johansson:

> With Parsifal in 1917 all Wagner's music dramas had reached the Royal Swedish Opera. Until the 1960s most of them were performed there every season, regularly given new productions. So several generations of Swedish artists were trained in a Wagnerian tradition with close ties to Bayreuth and to the great opera houses in Vienna, London and New York.

Great Swedish Wagner singers from the 1950s through the 1990s were Birgit Nilsson, Kerstin Meyer, Erik Saedén, Barbro Ericsson, Berit Lindholm, Bengt Rundgren, Catarina Ligendza, Helge Brilioth and Gösta Winberg, Johansson says. And as for contemporary names you could add Lars Cleveman, Nina Stemme and Katarina Dalayman.

This overview speaks for itself. It kind of makes you proud of being Swedish. And the pay-off Johansson delivers holds a promise for the future: "[T]he rebirth of Swedish Wagner singers now comes on with imposing speed, and the always controversial German musical dramatist is once again a central attraction of the Royal Swedish Opera with new productions of *Tannhäuser, Tristan und Isolde* and *Der Ring des Nibelungen.*"

So much for the Royal Swedish Opera and Wagner. You could add that in Sweden Wagner is also performed at the open air venue of Dalhalla in the county of Dalarna. It's a former stone quarry, an amphitheatre shaped cauldron on whose bottom the stage is placed. There's even a lake of greenish water nearby; the Rhine Maidens actually swam there when Dalhalla staged *The Rhine Gold* in 2013. The plans seem to be to stage all of The Ring there. In one word: promising.

ON SOURCES, TRANSLATIONS AND SPELLING

Hereby are presented some formalia on sources, translations and spelling. The comic poem cited at the beginning of chapter 1 is from the CBS compilation *Wagner's Greatest Hits* (1971). The rest of that chapter is, as hinted in the text, based on Lundewall, Jeanson and Mayer. Also, some facts have been gathered from Wikipedia [entry: Richard Wagner] in the footnotes. Overall in the text, when "Wikipedia" is mentioned I mean the English language Wikipedia articles and nothing else. If, for example, I say "according to Wikipedia [entry: Die Feen]", then I base the information on the English Wikipedia page thus captioned.

In this book I quote rather a lot from the German original libretti. Why German you might ask, why not in English? Because Wagner operas are sung in German, where ever they are staged. Also, English translations of the libretti are in circulation so you can check up on them if you wish to delve further into the opera texts. In this book, however, the English translations given of the Wagner libretti quotes are mine. They are, as noted in the text, free translations. The German originals are metric poetry, my renderings are of the more prosaic type. But I've amused myself with giving interpretations that are somewhat sensitive to the spirit of the original. And once I even got the meter right, in the Lohengrin Bridal Chorus. Otherwise, don't use my translations in order to sing. For this there are proper, metrical English translations available.

The Wagner libretti I have used are the ones issued by Sweden's Royal Opera in the 1960's and 1970's. I sometimes call the institution by the then proper Swedish moniker "Kungliga Teatern", which was the official name until 1997. From then on it's officially "Kungliga Operan", in daily usage simply "Operan". In English you of course can call it The Swedish Royal Opera or whatever.

In chapter 16, some of the info about Ludwig of Bavaria's building projects are from the BBC documentary "Fairytale Castles of King Ludwig II". The program had Dan Cruickshank guiding us through the buildings proper, in a serious, inspirational overview.

One of the sources for this study is Thomas Mann's *Wagner und unsere Zeit*. This book was edited after the death of its author, the German author Thomas Mann (1875-1955). It contains practically everything he has said on the subject of Wagner and Wagner's music, in letters, essays and the like. In an afterword the editor Erika Mann adds that there are also lines on Wagner in Mann's novels such as *Buddenbrooks*, *Tristan* and *Wälsungenblut* but they are not included in *Wagner und unsere Zeit*, these passages not being as easily anthologized.

As for translations from Swedish language biographies, essays etc. they are done by me, Lennart Svensson. That's what "translated by the author" means.

As for spelling the names of Edda texts and Asa gods in general I've striven to use the Icelandic original names. But sometimes I might have used Swedish name forms. As for the names of the Aesir in Wagner's plays proper I of course use the German names, such as Wotan, Fricka and Donner.

OPERA LIBRETTI

Das Rheingold (Rhenguldet). Kungliga teatern, Stockholm 1968
Der fliegende Holländer (Den flygande holländaren). Kungliga teatern, Stockholm 1977
Die Meistersinger von Nürnberg (Mästersångarna i Nürnberg). Kungliga teatern, Stockholm 1977
Die Valküre (Valkyrian). Kungliga teatern, Stockholm 1968
Götterdämmerung (Ragnarök). Kungliga teatern, Stockholm 1970
Lohengrin (Lohengrin). Kungliga teatern, Stockholm 1974
Parsifal (Parsifal). Kungliga teatern, Stockholm 1971
Siegfried (Siegfried). Kungliga teatern, Stockholm 1969
Tristan und Isolde (Tristan och Isolde). Kungliga teatern, Stockholm 1970

VIDEOS

Mithec Video Classics: *In the Eye of the Ring*. Centre Cuturel des Capucins and Bibliotheque Nationale de France. [No publication year is given.]
Leith, Alexander (producer and director): *Fairytale Castles of King Ludwig II*. BBC4, London 2013

LITERATURE

Adorno, Theodor: *Versuch über Wagner*. München 1964
d'Annunzio, Gabriele: *Elden*. Natur & Kultur, Stockholm 1946 (Italian original, *Il Fuoco*, 1900. An English translation was called *The Flame of Life*.)
Evans, Richard J: *The Coming of the Third Reich*. London 2004
Evans, Richard J: *The Third Reich in Power*. The Penguin Press 2005
Evola, Julius: *The Mystery of the Grail: Initiation and Magic in the Quest for the Spirit*. Inner Traditions, Rochester, Vermont, 1996. 208

pages. (*Il mistero del Graal e la tradizione ghibellina dell'Impero*, 1938)
Faye, Guillaume: *Archeofuturism*. Arktos 2010 (French original 1998)
Fest, Joachim: *Hitler*. Berghs, Malmö 1974 (German original: *Hitler – Eine Biographie*, 1973)
Gustafsson, Lars: *Tennisspelarna*. Norstedts 1977 (English version as *The Tennis Players*, 1983)
Hitler, Adolf: *Mein Kampf* (1926). English 1941 version, *My Struggle*, on Internet Archive.
Jeanson, Gunnar and Rabe, Julius: *Musiken genom tiderna, del 3*. Gebers 1967
Kubizek, August: *Adolf Hitler, mein Jugendfreund*. Graz/Göttingen 1953
Mann, Thomas: *Wagner och vår tid*, Norstedts, Stockholm 1968. (German original, *Wagner und unsere Zeit*, 1963.)
Mayer, Hans, *Richard Wagner*. Cete, Borås 1980 (German original on Rowohlt 1959)
Nietzsche, Friedrich: *Der Fall Wagner* (1888). Dtw 1999
Nietzsche, Friedrich: *Ecce Homo* (1888). Dtw 1999
Rauschning, Hermann: *Gespräche mit Hitler*. Zürich/Wien/New York 1940
Rosell, Ingrid: *Spegling av en värld*. Fischer & Co 1987
Spotts, Frederick: *Bayreuth: A History of the Wagner Festival*. Yale University Press 1999.
Wagner, Richard: *My Life (Mein Leben)*. Part II: 1850-1864 (1870). English translation, in the form published in New York 1911, online on Gutenberg.org

ABOUT THE AUTHOR

Lennart Svensson (born 1965) made his debut in 2007 with the short story collection *Eld och rörelse* (in Swedish only, but the title translates as *Fire and movement*). In 2009 he published the novel *Antropolis*, about which Joakim Andersen of the Swedish think-tank Motpol wrote: "A fascinating and readable novel, a combination of a novel of ideas and a vision of the future." In 2014 Manticore Press published Svensson's biography of Ernst Jünger, *Ernst Jünger – A Portrait*. About this book Living Traditions Magazine said: "A biography of the very highest calibre." Other than this Svensson in Swedish has published short stories, magazine articles and e-books. Moreover, since 2007 he blogs at The Svensson Galaxy. He lives in Härnösand on the northern Swedish coast. He also has a BA in Indology.

www.ingramcontent.com/pod-product-compliance
Lightning Source LLC
Chambersburg PA
CBHW061308110426
42742CB00012BA/2106